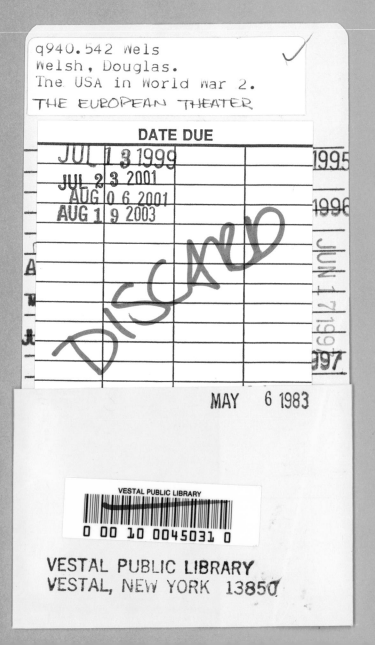

THE USA IN
WORLD WAR 2

THE USA IN WORLD WAR 2

THE EUROPEAN THEATER

DOUGLAS WELSH

Galahad Books · New York City

 A Bison Book

First Published in the US by
Galahad Books
a division of A & W Publishers, Inc.
95 Madison Avenue
New York
New York 10016

Copyright © 1982 Bison Books Limited

Produced by
Bison Books Limited
4 Cromwell Place
London SW7

Library of Congress Catalog Card Number
81-86652

ISBN 0-88365-602-7

Printed in Hong Kong

CONTENTS

1 THE ARSENAL OF DEMOCRACY

On 7 December 1941 the United States was thrust into war by the Japanese attack on Pearl Harbor. America was shocked and horrified by this event, not least of all because it was not the direction from which American leaders anticipated an overt attack. Throughout and in the aftermath of the Great Depression, which spread its influence worldwide, the United States watched the rise of three major dictatorships. Hitler's Germany, Mussolini's Italy and the Imperial military dictatorship in Japan presented growing threats to world security. The courses set by Germany and Italy most directly threatened peace in Europe and consequently the United States. Although aggressive gestures were being made by Japan, the United States and European nations with interests in the Pacific were confident in their ability to gauge the capabilities of the Japanese Empire. The vastness of the Pacific and Asia was considered a great barrier to Japan's struggle for power which gave the United States a false sense of security. Little attention was therefore paid to Japan's activities as the United States focused on developments in Europe. On the European continent all that separated the nations were their borders and the treaties and armies which protected them. It was the immediacy of the possibility of armed conflict which differentiated Europe from the Pacific. The volatility of Europe created the subtle shift in American foreign policy toward the affairs of that continent.

In 1933 the United States recognized the Soviet Union and its Communist government. Initially that recognition was prompted by economic factors. An increase in trade with the Soviet Union would aid in the economic recovery of the United States. However the establishment of a working relationship with the Soviet Union, including treaties, would prove beneficial in the event of confrontation with the rising expansionism of Japan. The Soviet Union recognized these advantages and agreed to halt propaganda activities against the United States to achieve a bond between the two nations. That agreement was short-lived. At that same time the United States decided to set its own house in order by initiating its 'good neighbor' policy toward the Latin American nations. President Franklin Delano Roosevelt led the campaign by pledging the United States to a policy of non-interference in Latin American affairs. He urged American businesses with assets in Latin America to

Left: President Franklin Delano Roosevelt.
Above: Admiral William Leahy was Roosevelt's Chief of Staff from 1942.
Above right: gasoline was in restricted supply in the US from August 1941.

deal directly with the Latin American governments and to negotiate with those governments rather than expect the United States forcibly to protect their rights. In various ways Roosevelt worked to ensure that Latin American governments did not become sympathetic to other foreign governments which might in the future be hostile to the United States. By encouraging an atmosphere of understanding and cooperation rather than belligerence and interference Roosevelt was securing America's borders against adversaries in the Western Hemisphere. War in Europe seemed inevitable. He did not want to have to worry about threats from across his southern borders as well.

By 1934 the United States began to broaden its amiable relations with other nations by reducing existing tariffs, often by as much as 50 percent. A 'most favored nation' clause was established to promote trade and trust between the United States and those governments with which it was considered prudent to maintain favorable relations. Under this policy new trade and tariff agreements were established with Great Britain, Canada and others. Cooperation in trade was also laying the foundation for future

political cooperation if the need arose by providing its economic foundation.

Although the United States was moving quietly on a course which laid the first steps for treaties and alliances which could draw America into war, it must be remembered that a deep-rooted isolationist policy had been regenerated after World War I. The primary cause of the return to isolationism was the disillusionment felt by the American people. The Great War, the war to end all wars, had not brought democracy, freedom, disarmament or lasting peace. The petty bickering of the European nations had resumed immediately. The unfair, vengeful Treaty of Versailles, the armaments race and European tariff wars were clear indications that Europe would continue on its long-established course. President Woodrow Wilson's Fourteen Points, acclaimed by many as a means to lasting peace and as guidelines for a new beginning, had been discarded and ignored. Wilson's concept of the League of Nations, adopted by many governments, was failing. The fact that the United States had refused to join the League contributed to undermining its potential, but most importantly the League lacked authority to do more than verbally reprimand those nations whose actions were not conducive to world harmony. Often, rather than be publicly condemned, representatives would simply walk out of the League conferences. It was in fact the unwillingness of any nation to see beyond its own interests which doomed the League to failure.

Another factor which influenced the disillusionment of the American people was the report issued by the Senate Munitions Investigation Committee in 1934. It was suggested that many American bankers and munition manufacturers had engaged in war profiteering. Not only did they make enormous profits, but it was generally agreed that the protection of the monetary interests of these groups in Europe was influential in drawing the United States into World War I. Although there were those who strongly disagreed with this statement, at the time the Committee's findings merely reaffirmed the isolationist, pacifist position. Young Americans, convinced of the futility of war as an effective means of change and disgusted by the senseless waste of life, were drawn to these positions.

There were two other factors which influenced and reaffirmed the isolationist stance. One was the Great Depression. Most Americans considered economic recovery as a monumental task toward which the government should focus all its attention and resources. Until stability was achieved in the United States, few Americans had any inclination to concern themselves with affairs in Europe or Asia. Another factor was the security afforded the United States by its geographical position. The two largest natural barriers in the world, the Pacific and Atlantic Oceans, separated the United States from its potential enemies in Europe and Asia. The promotion of friendly relations with Central and South Americas confirmed this sense of security, giving rise to the belief that the United States could remain aloof from the strife that threatened to engulf Europe once again.

In 1934 the isolationists achieved a great victory toward the maintenance of their position when Johnson's Debt Default Act was passed by Congress. Fundamentally the Act stated that neither the American Government, businesses nor private citizens could lend money to any country which had failed to repay its World War I war debts to the United States. As this included several prominent nations the isolationists believed that the act would ensure that the United States would not again be drawn into war to protect loans or investments made abroad.

In the years which followed, political and military upheavals around the world promoted the addition of neutralist sentiments to the isolationist. As Americans became increasingly concerned with their country's relationships with other governments, neutralist legislation was introduced in Congress. In the period between 1935 and 1937 three important neutrality acts were adopted. The first prohibited the sale of munitions to warring or belligerent nations. As this act did not make distinctions between friend and foe, it tied the hands of the Roosevelt Administration in offering assistance to those nations considered to be in harmony with American policy. The second act in the series gave the President the power to list those commodities, other than munitions, which could be sold to warring or belligerent nations on a 'cash and carry' basis. Any items listed by the President which might justifiably be considered contraband would generally have to be transported on vessels belonging to the purchasing government, not on American vessels. If for any reason an United States vessel was transporting such items, that vessel was prohibited from entering any port in a designated war zone. This issue of contraband transportation had been a point of major contention prior to World War I and a great deal of controversy was intended to be avoided in this manner.

The third act was perhaps the most controversial, as it prohibited American citizens from traveling on vessels of warring or belligerent nations. Although there were those who balked at this act as a limitation of personal freedoms, the neutralists cited the *Lusitania* as an example of the ramifications of such travel. This particular Act must surely have struck a nerve with President Roosevelt. As is now being explained, there were unusual circumstances surrounding the loss of the *Lusitania*. These circumstances seem to imply that the acting American Secretary of the Navy in 1915, Franklin Delano Roosevelt, and his counterpart at the British Admiralty, Winston Churchill, acted both directly and indirectly to influence the events which led to that disaster. This influence includes the mysterious redirection of escort vessels from the *Lusitania* and the attempt to hide the fact that the *Lusitania* was carrying munitions.

Freedom of the seas was considered forfeit through this final act, but the neutralist atmosphere had prevailed. The possible dangers and effects of permitting American citizens to travel on foreign vessels or to foreign countries which were potentially hostile were too great. However this limitation of personal freedom provoked a backlash in American society. It was in effect the final straw in what a growing percentage of the population saw as an unhealthy course in American policy. This regulation, linked with Roosevelt's New Deal, gave rise to claims that government was becoming too restrictive, too involved in legislating the lives of individuals. The combination of the three acts also resulted in accusations that the United States Government was taking an ostrich-like, head-in-the-sand approach to the world situation. In refusing to judge right or wrong or distinguish ally from enemy it was alleged that Roosevelt's Administration was shirking its inter-

Below: two P-51 Mustang pilots of the all-negro 332nd Fighter Group, which operated in Italy.
Bottom: two negro Marines walk through Harlem.

taking a responsible position in the international community. He had realized that it would be difficult to rally support in any other direction until stability was achieved. But by late 1937 FDR believed that the climate was beginning to change and that he could no longer afford to remain silent on such major issues. His speeches began to reflect the shift in sentiment as he took a more positive stance against aggression. In October 1937 Roosevelt made his famous Quarantine Speech. He likened the growing hostility in Europe to a disease. He stated that nations which took part in hostile or belligerent activities spread the contagious disease and should therefore be segregated from the remainder of the world by political and economic methods until such time as they could demonstrate that they had overcome their sickness. As other nations were similarly affected by the need for

national responsibility to the victims of overt aggression. This anti-neutralist or anti-isolationist movement which gained momentum after 1937 demanded that the United States take a stand against the hostile climate which was rapidly spreading around the world.

President Roosevelt agreed with this position. Until 1937 FDR made little effort to oppose the neutrality laws although he personally had a clear image of the role that the United States should play in

economic recovery Roosevelt believed that such restrictions would provide a deterrent. The United States would quickly be given an opportunity to test this theory.

In December 1937 the Panay Incident occurred. The American gunboat USS *Panay* was bombed and strafed by Japanese aircraft on the Yangtze River in China. Three American oil tankers were also attacked. Several American crewmen were killed and a number more wounded. The sanctions which might have been

Above: GIs of the 92nd Division in Italy, September 1944.
Right: accommodation aboard troopships was very cramped.

brought against Japan in the wake of Roosevelt's quarantine concept were avoided when the Imperial Government offered the United States a full apology, compensation and assurances that such an incident would not occur again. This satisfied the American people in their anxious attempt to avoid confrontation. Of Americans polled after the incident 60 percent stated that they not only believed in the acceptance of Japan's apology but also that they thought the United States should withdraw from China to avoid future confrontations with Japan.

By 1938 the United States was beginning to encounter genuine difficulties in its bid to maintain a neutral stance. The Spanish Civil War was expanding and Japan attacked the entire coastline of China with renewed intensity. The fascist dictators Hitler and Mussolini intervened in Spain, sending volunteers and equipment to support General Franco, while the Soviet Union bolstered the Spanish Republic. The United States joined with England and France in a policy of non-intervention. Roosevelt followed the neutralist policy established by the government by banning the shipment of goods which could be even remotely considered as contraband to any of the parties involved in the Spanish conflict.

In the midst of this concern in international politics

Germany invaded Austria in a bloodless takeover on 11 March 1938. Two days later an *Anschluss*, the union of Austria and Germany, was declared. Six months later Hitler demanded the surrender of the Sudeten region of Czechoslovakia, known also as the Sudetenland, to Germany. Hitler claimed that this region had been unjustly stolen from Germany and that its large German speaking population must be returned to the Fatherland. Czechoslovakia possessed one of the most well-trained armies of the time and the incident might have led to open conflict in Europe had it not been for the Munich Agreement. British Prime Minister Neville Chamberlain and French Premier Edouard Daladier signed a pact with Hitler and Mussolini accepting the German demands on the Sudeten and foresaking Czechoslovakia, whom both England and France might have been expected to protect Chamberlain, returning from the Munich conference, proclaimed that England and France had secured 'peace in our time.' In the naive desperation for peace and continued isolationism the American people accepted Chamberlain's assessment, but there were many who condemned the quiet acceptance of the German expansionism as a prelude to war.

Throughout this time Roosevelt had not remained idle. His acknowledged interest in the United States

Navy aided him in gaining Congressional approval for a one billion dollar appropriation for a 'two ocean' fleet in January 1938. In various speeches, primarily one given in August 1938, Roosevelt reiterated the American dedication to the Monroe Doctrine. On that occasion he specifically indicated America's respect for the sovereignty of Canada, expressing the position that any attempt by any nation to violate that sovereignty would be considered an act of war against the United States. In December the Pan American Union met to agree upon action to be taken in the Western Hemisphere. Roosevelt extended the position taken with Canada to all members of the Union. It was becoming evident that Roosevelt was guiding the country toward a more internationally oriented policy. As such increases in national defense would soon be forthcoming.

In January 1939 President Roosevelt addressed Congress and the nation in his annual State of the Union message. He examined the world situation urging Congress to reexamine the 1935–37 neutrality acts and to consider larger appropriations for all branches of the armed services. Although a sense of urgency was being felt and proclaimed Roosevelt knew he faced a difficult road ahead. It would require many more acts of aggression by Germany, Italy and Japan before Congress or the American people would be moved to abandon their isolationist stance. The President's worst fear was that open conflict would erupt in Europe and the United States would be unprepared to give aid.

On 15 March 1939 as Congress considered the requests made by the President, Hitler's armies took all of Czechoslovakia. One month later Mussolini ordered Italian troops into Albania. Although these circumstances took England and France somewhat by surprise, both countries realized that there was little they could do short of declaring war on Germany and Italy. Even in the face of such aggression the thought of war was so unpopular that the English and French governments' reaction was to announce the criteria for war. They stated that if Germany made any aggressive move toward Poland a state of war would then exist between England and France and Germany. In the following weeks both countries attempted to draw the Soviet Union into the Polish agreement. In August it was finally realized that the Soviet Union's reluctance to adopt the position set by England and France was a result of the secret non-aggression pact Stalin had made with Hitler. That pact freed Hitler from the threat of a two front war and opened the way for his next move.

On 1 September 1939 German troops struck Poland and two days later Great Britain and France declared war on Germany. The war for which the United States was not prepared was a reality. Roosevelt lost no time in moving to aid England and France. On 21 September he called for a special session of

Above: Hitler makes his triumphant entry into Danzig in September 1939. The United States kept aloof from the European war which Hitler's aggression against Poland precipitated.
Below: the 'Phony War' was the comparative lull between the crushing of Poland and the German *Blitzkrieg* in the West. German propaganda slogans are directed at French troops.

Congress to amend the 1937 Neutrality Act. Roosevelt explained that while the act might keep the United States safely out of war the embargo of materiel to belligerent nations was actually aiding Germany. England and France were in desperate need of supplies. American refusal to aid these friendly nations was a gross injustice to the victims of German aggression. After six weeks of debate a compromise solution was reached with the Arms Embargo Act. This legislation established a policy of materiel and munitions sales to a select group, although American vessels were not permitted to carry these 'contraband' goods. In October delegates to the Panama Conference declared a 300 to 1000 mile safety zone around North, Central and South America into which armed vessels of any of the belligerent nations could not enter. This declaration was challenged not only by Germany but by Britain and France. Yet the United States and Western Hemisphere nations, although sympathetic to the Allies' position, made it clear that they wanted to keep the war well away from the Americas.

Although on 3 September 1939 Britain and France entered the war it was known as the Phony War, as hostility existed but little fighting was actually taking place. Neither Britain nor France were willing to invade Germany. The situation in Poland was impossible. The Soviet Union had joined Germany in attacking that nation, occupying land taken from them by post-World War I treaties. However in April 1940 the Phony War that had become the object of ridicule exploded as the German armies turned to attack Western Europe. In a matter of weeks German military might overran Denmark, Norway, the Netherlands, Belgium, Luxembourg and Northern France. On 26 May the British Expeditionary Force which had been stationed in France was evacuated through Dunkirk with those French, Dutch and Belgian forces who could also escape. By 10 June Western Europe had virtually collapsed. Mussolini declared war on the Allies dragging Italy into conflict with England and France. Italy visualized itself as the military power of the Mediterranean, but its campaign into France would prove disastrous.

By 22 June 1940 France had been conquered by German armies and an armistice was signed. The French National Committee, known as the Free French and commanded by General Charles De Gaulle, pledged to continue resistance against the German occupation in spite of the capitulation of the government. France was duly divided. The northern region fell under direct German occupation while the central and southern areas, Vichy France, were governed by a puppet government headed by Marshal Pétain. Although the Free French labeled Vichy officials and sympathizers as traitors, Pétain and his supporters saw Vichy France as a compromise to keep some degree of French control over their nation rather than having the entire country ravaged by the Germans.

Before France fell Winston Churchill became Prime Minister of Britain. Churchill realized that for the moment the war on the Continent was lost, but he moved quickly to rally the British Empire and to negotiate with the United States for assistance. As Churchill looked to the United States, it too was considering the measures needed to strengthen and secure its defense. During the summer and fall of 1940 one of the first reactions of Congress was the passage of the Smith Act. This legislation tightened the control of the government over aliens residing in the United States and made it illegal for any resident to advocate the overthrow of the United States Government or to belong to any organization which professed such sentiments. Also during those months a gathering of North and South American delegates met in Havana, Cuba, to discuss the defense and protection of the Western Hemisphere against possible German aggression. One of the most notable agreements to emerge from this conference was that which stated that the United States was to take responsibility for colonies in the Western Hemisphere which belonged to any of the involved belligerent European nations. Such colonies were to be held in trusteeship by the nations of the Americas until the end of the war when they would then be returned to their rightful governments. In so doing the delegates hoped to reduce the possibility of the war expanding into their hemisphere under the aegis of colonial interest.

Two weeks after the Havana meeting Roosevelt met with Prime Minister King of Canada to discuss the creation of a permanent joint board for the defense of the North American continent. Responsibility for that defense would rest with those two nations. Finally after much debate the Burke-Wadsworth Act was passed and signed into law by President Roosevelt in mid-September 1940. This act, commonly known as the Draft Act, required all men between the ages of 21 and 35 to register for service in the armed forces. Those inducted under the act were liable for one year of active service and training then a period of reserve status. Thus by the end of 1940 American defensive awareness and preparedness was gathering momentum.

One area in which Roosevelt could not be satisfied was in the aid being given to potential allies, particularly Britain. In his annual message of January 1941 he asked the American people and Congress to proclaim the United States the 'Arsenal of Democracy.' In so doing not only would the United States begin a massive defense program to equip itself, but would lend or lease military equipment to the British or any other nation caught in the war against oppression. Controversy over Roosevelt's lend-lease proposal erupted immediately. The arguments followed two basic lines. Those who agreed

Below: United States' troops disembark in Iceland in 1942, while *en route* to Europe.
Right: Roosevelt and Churchill pictured aboard HMS *Prince of Wales* in August 1941. Their meeting resulted in the Atlantic Charter. Behind the leaders are General Marshall (left) and Admirals King and Stark.
Far right: US paratroops check their equipment during preparations for the invasion of Sicily.

with the President claimed that it was wise to provide armaments to Britain so that it might have the means to bring the war to a swift, favorable conclusion before the United States could be drawn into it. The opposing argument was based on the belief that if the United States took so active a role on behalf of one side in the conflict the other side would construe this as belligerent interference which would draw the United States into the war. With pressure from the Roosevelt Administration, Congress passed the Lend Lease Act of March 1941. Seven billion dollars were appropriated to make available war materials, such as ships, aircraft and tanks, to Britain and its allies. Later in June 1941 when Germany invaded the Soviet Union, Lend Lease was extended to Stalin's government in spite of the fact that there were those who well remembered the Poland issue of the previous year.

As the Lend Lease program got into full swing the United States was faced with a problem similar to that encountered in World War I. Submarines, both German and Italian, were sinking large numbers of naval and merchant vessels. In the North Atlantic the dangers were particularly acute. In April 1941 US Navy vessels began trailing German and Italian submarines, radioing their positions to the British

Navy but taking no direct action against the U-Boats. In July a contingent of American troops was stationed in Iceland, primarily to prevent Germany from establishing bases there. Iceland was an integral part of the North Atlantic naval protection system, particularly as a base for naval patrol aircraft. In August President Roosevelt announced the adoption of Atlantic Charter. Based on the common principles of Wilson's Fourteen Points, the Charter committed the United States to the policy of protecting the world from aggressive, hostile governments. It was at this point that Roosevelt truly began his undeclared war against Germany.

By September 1941 Roosevelt considered the submarine dilemma so critical that he issued orders for US Navy warships to shoot on sight any German or Italian submarine found within the safety zone which had been established during the Panama Conference. During the same month the US Navy began to provide protection for merchant ship convoys as far as Iceland. Two months later Congress gave approval for American merchant vessels to begin carrying goods to England and permission for such vessels to enter established combat zones. Once these previous restrictions were lifted merchant vessels began to arm themselves. Regular Navy crewmen were

employed to augment merchant crews. The gradual increase of American involvement in European affairs was rapidly accelerating.

Throughout these months the United States was not free to focus all of its attention and efforts on Britain and Europe. The situation in the Pacific and Asia was becoming more urgent. The United States Government had long been sympathetic to the needs and welfare of China and, as Japan continued to expand its sphere of influence on the Asian continent, discord between the Imperial Japanese government and the United States grew. By July 1941 Roosevelt's displeasure was made evident in an embargo on shipments of petroleum products, machine tools, scrap iron and steel bound for Japan. Japanese assets in the United States were frozen. The following month Congress approved the extension of Lend Lease to China to give aid in its war with Japan. In November Japan sent a peace mission to the United States. Three Japanese demands were presented as conditions for securing peaceful coexistence. The United States was to unfreeze all Japanese assets, to resume the delivery of embargoed goods, primarily petroleum, and to cease all military aid to China and remove civilian or military personnel who were advising the Chinese

armed forces. The demands were unrealistic and although Roosevelt's Administration made several counterproposals none were acceptable to the Japanese delegates.

The American people awoke on Sunday 7 December 1941 to discover that in spite of peace negotiations the United States had been catapulted into war by a Japanese attack on Pearl Harbor. Roosevelt, whose primary concern had been for Europe, was caught off guard by the attack but asked Congress on 8 December for a declaration of war against Japan. Other nations with regional or colonial interests in Asia and the Pacific followed suit. The United States had no alternative but to declare war on Japan, but there was still no justifiable reason for American involvement in the European war. That circumstance would quickly change. On 11 December 1941 Hitler and Mussolini declared that their nations were at war with the United States. There was no valid reason for such a declaration at that time, though Hitler obviously sought to throw the United States into the chaos of a two front war in his alliance with Japan. In fact Germany's declaration of war allowed Roosevelt to initiate active plans for cooperation with Britain to defeat the Axis Powers.

2 THE CALL TO WAR

The Japanese attack on Pearl Harbor in December 1941 thrust Roosevelt into a situation that he had not anticipated. Although the United States had taken a tough stance against Japan on the China issue, FDR had geared his policies to respond to the growing conflict in Europe. In effect with declarations of war by Japan, Germany and Italy, the United States found itself faced with a two front war while having formulated a one front strategy. New strategies would have to be rapidly developed and grim realities faced. Japan's 'steam roller' conquests in Asia and the Pacific put the entire Pacific Theater in grave jeopardy of total collapse. The United States could not afford to delay its reaction, as of all the nations involved in the Pacific, only the United States had the resources to stabilize the situation. Committing those resources meant that a large proportion of American men and materiel would not be available to aid Britain in the war in Europe.

Perhaps more crucial to America's reaction was the simple fact that the United States was in no position to effect changes or apply pressure in Europe at this time. Although a draft act had been instituted the full mobilization of American manpower would take time. Large quantities of military equipment necessary for the training and combat use of American soldiers was essential. That and the demands of Lend Lease put a strain on industrial capabilities and until American manufacturing was fully mobilized concessions would have to be made. Thus Roosevelt had to choose whether he would delay the commitment of troops to any front until full resources could be brought to bear, or to engage early while American manpower was virtually untrained and industry struggled to meet the demands of war. The second policy might result in early defeats from which the United States would find it difficult to recover. With such limitations the United States had few options for immediate assistance to its allies in Europe. As had been the case in World War I the US Navy and merchant fleet was in the forefront as the nation's most adequately prepared service. The US Navy had already been providing convoy protection between the United States and Iceland in response to enemy attacks on American vessels. Therefore it would be the responsibility of American fleets to maintain lines of communication and keep supplies flowing to Britain until trained, equipped combat forces were ready.

The other strategic role open to the United States involved the Army Air Force. There was a distinct need for the United States to take some sort of offensive role against Germany and its allies. The morale of the American people would suffer otherwise. Britain had adopted a strategic bombing policy both as revenge for the German air attacks made on Britain and in an effort to weaken Germany. Such air attacks were costly in men and equipment, but American military experts believed that an offensive air policy would be the most productive means for early United States involvement in Europe. An American air force was created to assist RAF Bomber Command. Until full mobilization was achieved, allies in Europe would have to continue their land war without the assistance of American troops. Another factor which greatly effected the American ground combat policy in Europe was the fact that at this early stage only the Soviet Union was heavily engaged in land warfare. The British were only involved in combat in North Africa. Thus, when United States troops were finally committed to the war, North Africa would be their most logical destination. And finally, the explosive nature of the Pacific Theater with regard to its ramifications in the United States put a more urgent demand on American resources than the 'removed' European conflict.

As a result of the policy adopted by the Roosevelt Administration the methods by which the United States would become engaged in the war in Europe were of primary concern. In spite of Roosevelt's attempts to increase preparedness American land forces were caught off guard by the demands of modern warfare. When war was declared the US Army was composed of no more than five divisions and numbered approximately 200,000 officers and men. Of these five divisions not one could be considered battle ready. They were not at full strength nor did they possess adequate materiel or training for the task which lay ahead. At a time when it was

Right: a Sherman tank of the US 1st Armored Division pictured near Lucca in Italy on its way to the German Gothic Line defenses.

essential to build up the armed services, efforts to accomplish this were being curtailed. As the self-proclaimed Arsenal of Democracy the United States had virtually been stripped of essential equipment by the needs of its allies. As FDR chose not to impose reductions in the Lend Lease policy, during the first six months of the war American recruits found supplies of even the most obsolete weapons to meet training requirements inadequate. General Douglas MacArthur, one of the most outspoken opponents of Lend Lease, condemned the President for sending materiel to England and the Soviet Union while denying such areas as the Philippines. A prime example of this was that American Sherman medium tanks were persistently withdrawn from US Army units to resupply British armored divisions in North Africa. Although American generals voiced their disapproval, Army Chief of Staff and Chairman of the Joint Chiefs of Staff, General George C Marshall agreed with FDR's policy. As the hands of the nation were temporarily tied, it seemed logical to release American equipment to those who could put it to immediate use. In the long term the continuation of Lend Lease would save American lives as it allowed the United States' allies to continue to exert full pressure against the Axis in Europe.

General Marshall, in whom Roosevelt had complete confidence, was placed in command of American mobilization. Although many accused Marshall of failings in his role as a strategist, he had a keen ability to assess a situation and to develop appropriate strategies. He also had the ability to command the trust and respect of Allied generals, who firmly believed in Marshall's efforts to achieve the best for both the United States and its allies. Although aware of the need for materiel, Marshall was most concerned with the manpower issue. If not properly trained and led the millions of men destined for combat would be virtually worthless. The selection of candidates for officer and NCO ranks was of critical importance. There was no doubt in Marshall's mind that given qualified personnel the Infantry School at Fort Benning and the Command and General Staff school at Fort Leavenworth could produce officers and NCOs of a caliber equal to any other nation in the world. Marshall also placed great emphasis on close examination of regular army officers' field records and he achieved marked success throughout the war at having those promoted who best deserved it and at weeding out the incompetent and inept.

Another task facing Marshall involved the expansion of the five divisions with all possible speed while maintaining a high standard in each. By the end of the war Marshall had overseen the reconstruction of the American military machine. The Army alone had been increased to four army groups which incorporated nine armies or 23 corps. He had attained his goal of 89 divisions which were divided into 67 infantry divisions, 16 armor, five airborne and one cavalry division. The USAAF had grown to 12 air forces, totalling approximately 273 combat groups, with 7,600,000 men and 100,000 WACs in uniform. Although the juggling of men and materiel between Europe and the Pacific was a monumental task Marshall accomplished his mission with admirable success.

Through Marshall the General Staff had the foresight to adapt to the changes taking place in the art of warfare. The opening days of the European war clearly indicated that the German Blitzkrieg tactics were a recipe for victory. Mechanization and armor were no longer a luxury or elite unit concept. On the Eastern Front both Germany and the Soviet Union had massive mechanized formations, yet the bulk of the armies were still infantrymen who marched to keep pace with the fluid fronts. The essential transportation within these infantry units continued to be provided by horses. The American staff recognized the futility of the European formations. It was obviously pointless to possess the ability to burst through enemy lines and conquer territory with the lightning speed of mechanized units only to have the advance bogged down by the slow-moving infantry. The Europeans had long scoffed at the 'love affair' Americans had with gadgets and machines, but it was to answer an obvious need that all American divisions, whether armor or infantry, would be provided with sufficient vehicles for compatible mobility. American infantry divisions, which comprised approximately 14,000 men were issued with some 1500 vehicles. The emphasis on mobility illustrated the General Staff's desire to give the American ground troops every possible advantage in executing the strategies and tactics being formulated. Mechanization was to be the key to the rapid breakout of American forces in France in 1944 and would be the deciding factor in the ability of American commanders, primarily Patton, to save the Allies from defeat in the final German offensive.

As American divisions were created they followed the conventional organization, yet support units were added as an integral part of each division. By 1943 an American infantry division was composed of three infantry regiments of three battalions each and an artillery regiment with three groups of 105mm guns and one group of 155mm guns for a total of 48 artillery pieces. Also attached were an engineer battalion, a signals company and medical and supply units. It was the 1500 vehicles, often three or four times the number allotted to German divisions, which made the most obvious difference. Although American infantry divisions took a traditional form, armored divisions were quite another story. General Chaffee, with Marshall's support, developed a unique organizational program at the armor school at Fort Knox. Chaffee would play an integral role in the

Above: US troops fire their 60mm mortar. This weapon fired a
2.94lb projectile over a range of 1985 yards.
Above left: a standard US infantry weapon was the 0.30 caliber
Browning automatic rifle, which was fitted with a 20-round detachable
box magazine.
Left: the US Army's 57mm anti-tank gun was based on the British
6-pounder Mk2.

development of the United States armored strategy
and tactics. Armored divisions would consist of one
reconnaissance battalion of light tanks, four battalions
of medium tanks and three battalions of mechanized
infantry who rode in half-tracks thus allowing them to
carry larger quantities of heavy infantry weapons
within each unit. The division also possessed three
battalions of self-propelled 105mm howitzers, eigh-
teen in each battalion, and armor engineer battalion,
seperate assault engineer company and the usual
medical, maintenance and support units. Generally
the armor divisions established in the 1942–43 period
consisted of 160 M4 Sherman medium tanks, 68
Stuart light tanks, 68 armored cars and approximately
1200 wheeled, all-purpose vehicles which supported
and moved the division. The total divisional strength
of 230 tanks was in great contrast to the German
division strength of approximately 160 tanks. More-
over at the height of the war Germany could only
mount one battalion of infantry in each division in
halftracks while all accompanying American battalions were mechanized. The American self-propelled
guns mounted on tracked vehicles also gave increased
fire potential and mobility to the divisions over their
German counterparts. Unlike their European counterparts American armored divisions did not have
antitank or antiaircraft units. Although there was a
degree of antitank capability in the divisions such
support was usually allocated from higher commands
as the need arose.

There were other advantages to Chaffee's system.
The divisions could be easily broken down into
combat commands, flexible formations of tanks,
infantry and artillery supported by units of the
reconnaissance battalion. As the war progressed
armored divisions fell under the guidance of Combat
Command A and Combat Command B which were in
the field, while Combat Command Reserve acted as a
mobile reserve for the divisions.

Although the United States attempted to provide
its ground troops with the essentials of modern
warfare, American equipment was never quite able to
reach the quality of German materiel, except in the
basic infantry weapons. Infantrymen were armed
primarily with the semiautomatic rifle of M1 Garand
and M1 Carbine types whose high fire rate gave
American infantrymen an advantage on the battle-
field. Heavy infantry weapons included the BAR
(Browning Automatic Rifle), which was a 30 caliber,
air-cooled light machine gun. The BAR would prove
to be the most essential of the infantry company
support weapons. An improved version of the French
60mm mortar would also put a tremendous amount of
fire potential into the hands of company and platoon
officers.

The area in which the United States suffered most,
in spite of the advantages of the armored division, was
with its M4 Sherman tank. Although the Sherman
had an effective 75mm gun, it was never capable of
holding its own against the heavier German armor of

Left: Sherman tanks of the US Fifth Army's 752nd Tank Bn carry rocket guns atop their turrets.
Below: a mine roller Sherman tank of the US Sixth Army advances towards the River Moselle.
Right: Sherman tanks near St Vith, Belgium.

Below: a US 105mm howitzer mounted on an M-4 Sherman tank chassis.

the later war years. As a result a change in direction was made by the Americans and British, who relied on the American built tank. Rather than attempt to build a tank which could match the German equipment one for one, it was decided that it would be best to build reliable, capable tanks in larger quantities. The United States struggled to develop sufficient fire power to counter the Germans' heavy armor to support the tanks. It was soon realized that it was far better to rely on superior air support, which accounted for more tank 'kills' than any antitank unit could. Such tactical and strategic air support, furnished through the Allied air command, would see many changes throughout the war. However, the B-17 bomber would prove to be the mainstay of the American air war in Europe.

The most essential part of the American military machine, in spite of emphasis placed on mechanization, remained the infantryman, the GI. The average ground combat troop was 26 years of age. The ranks of the armed services would swell with new and first generation immigrants who rallied to the call of their adopted nation. Even those of German and Italian descent would take up arms against the dictators of their former homelands. One of the most surprising

and heroic units to fight in Europe was comprised of Japanese Americans or Nisei. American Indians would prove their full worth in the US Signal Corps. The army authorized these men to transmit messages in their tribal languages, thereby creating a 'code' which would baffle the Axis powers in Europe and in the Pacific throughout the war. Black Americans filled the ranks and although they first found themselves in the traditional roles of supply and maintenance several all Black combat units were formed in the Army and USAAF. Although racial prejudice was prevalent these men would be accorded respect for their valor on land and in the sky. When the montage of people of vastly different ancestral, social and economic backgrounds is considered, in conjunction with the fact that many were fighting against their former countrymen, a tribute must be paid to the adaptation of the American forces and to the patriotism displayed by their devotion to their new nation. In the midst of rapid training and preparation of the combat soldiers not even great emphasis on personal hygiene was overlooked. It was obvious that Marshall wanted the GI to be the most complete citizen-soldier the United States could produce. It was a crucial role. The fate of the world depended on him.

3 AT SEA AND IN THE AIR

As America mobilized for war it was forced to acknowledge that many months would pass before it could move beyond limited involvement in Europe. American reaction was therefore confined to several areas. As the 'arsenal of freedom' American industry had to keep pace with the demands made upon it. But the supply of materiel to Europe would become the task of the US Navy and merchant fleets. As such the war at sea was America's first true front in the European conflict. The Army Air Force was the only other military arm remotely capable of taking the war to the enemy in those early months.

When war was officially declared in December 1941 it merely expanded the possibilities open to the Navy. For more than one and a half years the United States had taken an increasing role in the European war. Through agreements made in 1941 the US Navy and Marines had become involved outside the secure zones of the Atlantic. Initial involvement was indirect, but as the Royal Navy felt the pressure of involvement in a global conflict the US Navy moved in to keep the Atlantic sealanes open. Iceland was the

site of more direct intervention. The German occupation of Denmark, on which Iceland was still dependent, forced a quick response. Iceland was a vital base which dominated the convoy routes across the North Atlantic. If Roosevelt's Lend Lease was to be effective the Atlantic sealanes had to be kept open.

The same agreement which resulted in US Navy and Marine personnel occupying Iceland also gave the US Navy the task of protecting American vessels on passage across the Atlantic. This policy was soon broadened to include vessels of any nationality which sought protection on the Atlantic. The United States defended this policy as non-belligerent, claiming that it had a right to maintain its lines of communication with Britain and to protect all nations' rights to freedom of the seas. But as the United States became more involved in the affairs of Europe, the likelihood of incidents with German or Italian submarines grew. In September the destroyer USS Greer was attacked by a U-Boat off the southern coast of Iceland. Although the Greer was not lost the attack caused repercussions in the United States. As had been the case with the *Panay* incident, apologies and assurances that such attacks would not be repeated were demanded. The Germans responded, as did the Japanese, but there was unease over the sincerity of that reply. The following month a U-Boat attacked and damaged the USS *Kearny*. The United States had lost its first casualties. This incident not only caused an outcry but gave Roosevelt just cause to give the US Navy *carte blanche* for the protection of lives and commodities at sea. This incident also led to a proposal that the United States merchant fleet should arm its vessels which Roosevelt approved.

When war finally came less than two months later Germany immediately dismissed the American chargé d'affaires and extended submarine warfare to include not only American vessels on the high seas, but also shipping off the United States coast. Of the 250 U-Boats less than 100 were actually involved in combat at a given time in the Atlantic, 55 of which roamed the North Atlantic. On 9 December before a formal declaration of war Admiral Doenitz, commander of U-Boat operations, launched Operation *Paukenschlag* (kettle-drum). Although Doenitz's plan was to destroy American shipping as quickly as possible, thus eliminating the trans-Atlantic lifeline of supplies, Hitler created problems for that strategy. He diverted all but five U-Boats from the Operation, though he would later release almost one dozen less modern submarines. Nevertheless Doenitz's plan would result in the destruction of thousands of tons of Allied shipping.

By January 1942 although the US Navy had several months of experience in antisubmarine warfare it continued to be outclassed. The United States was unprepared and that fact was reflected in performance. The defense of the east coast from Canada to Florida was the responsibility of the American Atlantic Fleet, commanded by Admiral R E Ingersoll who had succeeded Admiral King when he became Commander in Chief of US Fleets. Ingersoll, though given authority over the east coast defenses placed most of the responsibility for the mechanics of coastal defense on the shoulders of Vice-Admiral A Andrews. Andrews spent a great deal of time trying to explain the inadequacies of the coastal fleet to the government. Prior to war he warned that the United States was courting disaster in the Atlantic without the necessary development of both naval and air policies. He pointed out the need for strengthening the Atlantic fleet and coastal defenses and also the requirement for aircraft to patrol the sealanes and coastal waters. Without these changes in policy Andrews considered the task of protecting the Eastern Seaboard an impossibility.

In spite of Andrews' warnings there were many in power who believed that he was merely crying wolf. His fleet would consist of 12 surface vessels of World War I vintage and approximately 103 aircraft. Although on paper the aircraft strength appeared sufficient for the initial defense operations, of the 103 aircraft few were actually combat worthy. After war was declared the Army Air Force would be given operational duties along the coast to augment naval deficiencies. This would prove to be of questionable assistance as these pilots were not directly responsible to Andrews nor were they adequately trained in combined naval operations. They were in fact virtually useless in submarine search and attack. A typical air

Above left: the destroyer USS *Bainbridge* was one of the American escort vessels committed to the Battle of the Atlantic.
Right: USS *Kearny* at Reykjavik, Iceland, on 19 October 1941 showing the damage inflicted by a U-boat.

support operation after January 1942 involved three to six light bombers which would patrol some 600 miles of coastal waters twice each day. This in itself was inadequate but to make matters worse the USAAF commanders failed to realize that a change in flight patterns had to be made to prevent the enemy from evading regular air patrols. In his war memoirs Winston Churchill stated that when informed by the Admiralty of the conditions in the American Atlantic Fleet and coastal defenses he found the situation incomprehensible. Not only were the coastal defenses in chaos, but the United States had no plans for coastal convoys. Admiral King believed that the grouping of vessels when inadequate protection could be given was futile and that it was better to allow less conspicuous single ships to take their chances along the coast. Ingersoll agreed and warships were sent to sweep the Atlantic seaboard and Caribbean Sea, with negative results, while American merchant ships and oil tankers were sunk with regularity.

On 1 April the Secretary of the Navy announced that 28 U-Boats had been sunk by the Atlantic Fleet. This total was offset by the loss of nearly one million tons of American shipping sunk. It would later be claimed that the U-Boat figures had been drastically inflated with only eight or ten actually confirmed. The destroyer USS *Roper* was the first to achieve a U-Boat 'kill' on 14 January 1942, but the future months would prove that the German submarines would present more of a problem than the coastal defenses could handle.

One of the difficulties presented to the naval defenders was the lack of understanding of the nature of the threat to the east coast. In the early months of 1942 many ships were lost. Laxity in observing proper black-out procedures, the rigid adherence to pre-set courses and sea lanes and the uncoded radio transmission of air and naval positions by merchant vessels accounted for the ease with which U-Boats found their targets. American coastal towns and cities suffered similarly from that lack of understanding as they maintained a delusion that the war could not be brought to their doorstep. The bright lights of these cities made German navigation along the coast simple and more than one merchant vessel was lost after being sighted while silhouetted against the city lights. The dangers increased as Germany developed refueling vessels and procedures which gave the U-Boats the capability for sustained missions along the coast.

Throughout this period of error in the coastal defense a definite anti-British bias was noted not only by British Admiral Cunningham but by Winston Churchill. The bias was apparently rooted in the prejudice of Fleet Admiral King against the Royal Navy. As a result many tactics developed by the Royal Navy through trial and error were cast aside by King simply because they were British. Such concepts as convoys, search methods and combat tactics suggested

by the Royal Navy were ignored. Churchill went so far as to offer the United States Navy ten corvettes and twenty-four trawlers equipped with the most modern sonar submarine detection and interception devices in the hope that the United States would soon realize the seriousness of the situation. He included Royal Navy statistics on the losses which had and would be incurred unless the U-Boat threat was effectively dealt with. However there were other factors which influenced American reaction to the situation in the Atlantic. King was concerned to protect the resources being made available to the Pacific. The Lend Lease policy with the Soviet Union, the maintaining of a

relationship with Vichy France and the concerns of American mobilization did not effect Churchill or Great Britain, except as they drew American attention away from 'England's war.'

Although the opinions of Roosevelt's staff were divided General Marshall began to make suggestions and quietly changed the direction of the Navy. By May the Navy had begun to organize convoys for Atlantic merchant vessels and although efforts were made to safeguard the convoys losses increased. Marshall continued to bring pressure to bear on King for the development of more effective Atlantic policies. General Henry 'Hap' Arnold of the Army Air Force

was also brought into the planning to begin a more positive defense of the coastline and American shipping. This air activity would prove instrumental to the defeat of the U-Boat on the coast and in the Caribbean as eventually more than 600 aircraft, primarily light tactical bombers, patrolled the coast.

Although Marshall could not meet all of King's demands more equipment was sent to the Atlantic. That, combined with changes in naval tactics, altered the course of events. One technological advance was achieved by the application of sonar or ASDIC. Through the use of sonar, tactics were developed whereby convoy escort vessels would cooperate to trap and destroy the U-Boats. Although these tactics resulted in the loss of merchant vessels such losses were considered tolerable if the U-Boats were destroyed.

It was American industrial mobilization which truly swung the balance in Allied favor. By 1943 American shipbuilders were beginning to replace vessels almost as rapidly as the U-Boats could sink them. Allied raids against submarine bases on the coast of France increased U-Boat losses three-fold over the previous year. The German surface fleet was being countered with such success as to be virtually nullified, thus forcing a greater reliance on the U-Boat. This proved counter-productive, for although Admiral Doenitz might have added two years to the American struggle for superiority at sea, Hitler never gave him a free rein. It was not long until the U-Boats were forced to curtail their operations, patrolling the primary sea lanes, making it easier for Allied vessels to find and destroy them. German submarines would continue to be a menace until the end of the war but by 1943 their influence was waning.

By the end of the war 3000 Allied merchant ships and 145 combat vessels had been sunk in an effort to keep supplies and troops flowing across the Atlantic and Mediterranean Sea. The battle for the Atlantic unlike the Pacific surface battles would be a war of attrition. Once that war was won, through cooperation with the Royal Navy, the US Navy's role would primarily be to aid in the amphibious assaults for the invasions of North Africa and Europe.

As the Navy struggled with the U-Boats the air war was gathering momentum. The American Eighth Air Force stationed in England would become the United State's contribution to the Allied bomber offensive. Since the Battle of Britain RAF bombers had made a desperate bid to take the war to Germany. The bomber was Churchill's primary offensive weapon and although there were those who argued about the bombers' contribution to the war effort, Churchill viewed it as sustenance for the morale of Great Britain. The Americans saw it from the same perspective. Roosevelt recognized the opportunity presented by the air war to show American involvement in the war against the Axis. As the Doolittle Raid on Tokyo raised morale by taking the war to Japan the Eighth Air Force would take the war to Germany.

As had been the case with the Navy, early American-British relationships were not entirely congenial. Although RAF Bomber Command was well established and experienced, the USAAF in England was unwilling to relinquish its integrity to the British. The RAF strategy had concentrated on night area bombing when pin-point daylight bombing missions had proven too costly in men and aircraft. Both Britain and Germany had experimented with the latter concept and each had arrived at the same conclusion. As a result Bomber Command operated mainly at night. As Germany developed its night defense tactics and flak protection was extended to umbrella potential target areas, British bomber casualties increased in spite of the cover of darkness. When the American bomber commanders appeared on the scene they examined the British strategy and reached several conclusions. The first was that too much effort was being wasted in the approach taken by Bomber Command. Often four or five seperate missions were necessary to eliminate one target and even then success was limited. It was also apparent that darkness was not reducing losses to any great extent.

It was thus decided that although daylight bombing had been attempted new methods could make it more successful. One of the main differences in the American policy was made by the introduction of the top secret Norden bomb-sight in American bombers. By flying in a tight formation and delivering ordnance with accuracy the USAAF believed it could eliminate targets in one mission, thereby reducing casualties in the long term. Another advantage of American bombers was the additional armament with which they could defend themselves. The primary American bomber, the B-17, was appropriately named Flying Fortress. Both the B-17 and the B-24 Liberator were armed with heavy machine guns for the protection of their own aircraft as well as others in the formation. The B-17 had no less than thirteen 50 caliber machine guns mounted in turrets, hatchways and tail with a crew of ten men. The B-17 carried some 5000 pounds of bombs and had the potential strike range of 2100 miles. The B-24 Liberator although capable of carrying a larger payload had only ten 50 caliber machine guns. As the air war continued the Americans modified these aircraft, going to the lengths of developing a heavily-armed escort Fortress whose sole purpose was to act as long range defense for bomb-laden aircraft.

Although the British brought pressure to bear in the early days of the war for the American bombers to conform with RAF tactics, the Eighth Air Force commander General Ira Eaker fought to maintain his command's independence. He would cooperate with Bomber Command but General Eaker would 'call his own shots' in the daylight bombing strategy. On 17 August 1942 aircraft from the Eighth Air Force flew their first mission of the war. Twelve B-17s crossed the English Channel and attacked the German marshaling yards at Rouen. That first raid was a complete success with all aircraft returning safely to base. From then on the Eighth Air Force would progress to more important targets ever deeper into enemy territory. Churchill continued to harass Roosevelt in an effort to force the American air command to fall into line with established British policies. Churchill visualized combined American and British raids numbering several thousand bombers executing massive night attacks. General 'Hap'

Above: Consolidated B-24 Liberator bombers of the 376th Bomb Group fly over the Alps en route to targets in south Germany.

Arnold succeeded in preventing Roosevelt from agreeing to Churchill's demands.

As the British continued to raid such targets as the industrial Ruhr Valley and Berlin the American command followed a policy of selecting individual key targets for elimination. American accuracy was improving and repetitive missions were being reduced but American air casualties were mounting. The principle aim of target selection was the destruction of factories, rail yards and ports to eliminate German war production, particularly of aircraft. The most important reason for the failure of this ambition lay in the fact that German aircraft factories were located deep in Europe. The fact that Allied fighter range did not extend beyond the River Rhine made bomber missions deep into Germany more costly than productive.

As the war entered 1943 a crisis in the air war developed. Something had to be done to neutralize German fighter aircraft and that task fell to the USAAF. It was finally decided that if the German aircraft factories were inaccessible the key to the elimination of German air power was the destruction of selected related industries. If the scheme worked the Luftwaffe would be crippled and the American bombers would have a clear path for the destruction of other vital German industries. The first phase of the related aircraft industries strategy was the elimination of the ball-bearing factory in Schweinfurt. On 14 October 1943, 291 Flying Fortress bombers set out on the Schweinfurt Raid. Almost immediately upon the disappearance of Allied fighter protection, German fighter aircraft attacked. Although the B-17s pressed on and succeeded in causing some damage to the ball-bearing factory they felt the full weight of Luftwaffe fighter strength. Sixty bombers were lost and more than 130 sustained varying degrees of damage. Over the next week further operations against Schweinfurt resulted in 148 bombers and crews lost to the German air defenses. When these statistics were made known there was much criticism in the United States. General Arnold, in an effort to keep public opinion from turning against the air policy, portrayed the Schweinfurt Raid as a great success. He explained that losses of this magnitude were unavoidable if future combat losses were to be kept to a minimum. The simple fact was that the air war was having little effect on the German forces and the United States and Britain were ignoring this failure.

northern France. These missions would directly aid the preparations for an Allied invasion of Europe. Additionally the bombing of these areas would provide a breathing space during which Allied air losses could be recouped.

In spite of the change in direction Allied air commanders continued to look toward targets of strategic importance, especially German oil targets. When General Carl Spaatz assumed command of the Eighth Air Force in England and the Fifteenth Air Force in Italy on New Year's Day 1944 oil-related targets became of supreme importance. If the Americans or British could demonstrate that Germany's natural and synthetic oil supplies were in jeopardy then the bulk of German fighter aircraft would be allocated to the defense of those supplies. The result would be a reduction in fighter defense over other areas as the Luftwaffe centralized its operations. Although the British would continue to view strategic bombing of Allied cities as the deciding factor, Spaatz was convinced that this new strategy would prevail.

Early 1944 was a time of other changes. Between December 1943 and March 1944 the American P-51 Mustang long-range fighter aircraft was taking its place in the Eighth Air Force. The Mustang had the range to accompany American bombers from their bases in England as far as Berlin. German fighter aircraft were no longer able to dominate their skies and by March 1944 the balance had swung in the Allies' favor. The protection given by the Mustang reduced American air losses by more than 60 percent of those incurred six months earlier. Ground advances made by Allied forces played an important role in the air war success. As ground forces advanced in Italy and northern Europe bases were being denied to Germany and made available to Allied aircraft. This in turn provided greater range for Allied fighters and bombers, which could strike at areas previously denied them.

By the end of 1944 strategic bombing was having a destructive effect on German oil production. Surprisingly German production in other areas of manufacturing was at its highest levels. It was becoming obvious however that ground activity by the Russians on the Eastern Front and the American and other Allies on the Western Front was accomplishing what Allied bombing had failed to do. To destroy a factory was one thing but to take the ground on which it stood could not be accomplished from the air. As the war dragged on into 1945 the Allies would dominate the skies over Germany, continuing in their effort to reduce manufacturing to rubble and destroy the will to fight. In the final analysis the air war served as a morale booster for the Allies and it helped to soften the course of the actual invasion of Europe. It had not and could not bring victory on its own as many had thought it would.

Above: a bombadier mans his station in the nose of a Boeing B-17G Flying Fortress. The chin-mounted gun turret was introduced on this version to counter head-on fighter attacks.
Above far left: Col Don Blakeslee pictured in his P-51 Mustang.
Above left: Eighth Air Force B-17 Flying Fortresses.
Left: a P-51 Mustang escort fighter of the Eighth Air Force.

The year 1943 saw continued Bomber Command raids on populated areas such as Berlin and Hamburg. Hamburg alone was subjected to four nights of continuous RAF bombing, with smaller American raids which would take a large toll in lives both on the ground and in the air. The Schweinfurt Raid had marked the beginning of a time of failure for the Allied air war. A change in the policies was needed. That change was considered a shift back to reality and flexibility by many combat commanders after an extended period of rigid single-mindedness. The new strategy was simple. The RAF and the US Army Air Force would transfer efforts from massive attacks against Germany to the destruction of targets in

4 LIGHTING THE TORCH

As 1942 drew to an end the United States prepared for its first land invasion in the European Theater. From their earliest meetings after the declaration of war Roosevelt and Churchill realized the limitations set on both. Although they wanted to take the war as quickly as possible to the enemy the means of doing so was the subject of much debate. Many views were expressed, including an invasion of northern Europe, but considerable preparation would have to be made before such an operation could take place. The area which appeared most advantageous for initial American ground involvement was North Africa. There the British had been fighting a seesaw war with the Germans for control of this strategic Mediterranean region. Churchill and Roosevelt agreed that to introduce American ground infantry to war in North Africa would be economical in men, time and materiel. North Africa was also a likely area for Allied success.

As the months of 1942 rolled by and the United States began to mobilize, Allied Intelligence made known several facts which led to the decision to invade North Africa. The capabilities of Field Marshal Erwin Rommel and his Afrika Korps were becoming legendary and from the aspects of terrain and weather North Africa presented many problems. Yet as the Russian Front absorbed German troops it became increasingly evident that Hitler saw North Africa as a mere sideshow, sending as little as possible in front line equipment to that region. Both Britain and the United States saw the landings in North Africa as a means to bring France into the Allied camp once again. Morocco and Algeria were held by French forces and if these areas could be liberated it was believed that the French forces would put themselves under Allied command with the promise that they would soon participate in the liberation of France itself. It was thought that the French in North Africa sought only an excuse to unite with the Allies and that Vichy control would disintegrate once the Allies demonstrated their ability to defeat the Germans in Africa. Churchill also saw the need to open the Mediterranean to Allied shipping so that the long voyage around the Cape could be eliminated.

As time went on after the Arcadia Conference Roosevelt became more convinced of the wisdom of a North African invasion, but some American com-

manders held a less optimistic view. Members of the Joint Chiefs of Staff particularly General Marshall saw the North African landings as a waste of American resources and effort which, if undertaken at all, should be nothing more than a secondary operation. These men were concerned lest the North African operation deplete the stockpiles being made in anticipation of the European invasion. The US Chiefs of Staff might have been against the idea, but a majority of the Allied Combined Chiefs of Staff were very much in favor of the North Africa operation.

By April 1942 American industry was demonstrating its ability to provide adequate supplies and materiel for the eventual invasion of France. The success of this mobilization, code named Bolero, proved that supplementary equipment and supplies could easily be diverted to North Africa. Added to this was the assessment that it would be at least 1943, if not 1944, before the Allies' manpower pool was sufficient for a European invasion. There seemed little doubt that the North Africa invasion would receive high priority in spite of the objections raised in the American command structure. At one point the Joint Chiefs of Staff even suggested that Roosevelt shelve the North Africa issue and funnel all available resources to the Pacific. However by July 1942 Roosevelt had made his decision and ordered the Joint Chiefs of Staff to make preparations for the execution of Operation Torch, the invasion of North Africa.

In August 1942 it was decided that Lieutenant General Dwight D Eisenhower would command Operation Torch. To accomplish his task Eisenhower created Allied Forces Headquarters (AFHQ) combining British and American planners and staff in an invasion planning committee. In this way both British and American objectives could be given equal consideration and compromises made. Eisenhower quickly discovered that compromise would be a major factor in the planning of Torch. The British wanted their invasion force to land in Algeria, somewhere near Bône, so that they might rapidly deploy eastward into Tunisia. If Tunisia was secured the Germans would be unable to use it as an exit point to Sicily. The American staff was concerned with the possibility of Spanish intervention in the theater, or that Spain might open its airfields to the Luftwaffe. This could

Above: US troops land near Casablanca at the start of Torch.
Above left: Lt Gen Eisenhower commanded the Torch Operation.
Below: the Vichy leaders Pétain (left), Darlan and Laval.

jeopardize not only the invasion itself, but also the naval resupply of the ground forces in Algeria. The American strategy called for an invasion further west in Morocco.

A complicating factor was the delicate issue of the French administrations and forces in Morocco, Algeria and Tunisia. If the French should side with the Germans and offer heavy resistance it could create severe repercussions on the morale of the Allied forces. Eisenhower realized that the American people believed in the destruction of the Axis dictators and in lifting the 'yoke of oppression' from occupied European nations. If French forces in North Africa remained unwaveringly loyal to the puppet Vichy government and stood against the invasion the moral justification of the Allied war effort would be in serious doubt.

In an attempt to avoid this possibility secret negotiations were held with the Vichy politicians and commanders in the area. These negotiations had little success in the unstable political atmosphere. AFHQ went on with its planning in spite of this dilemma. It was finally decided that three invasion task forces, the Western, Center and Eastern Task Forces, would

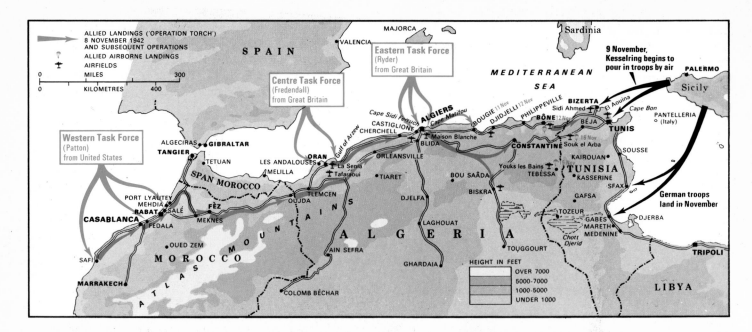

ALLIED LANDINGS ('OPERATION TORCH')
8 NOVEMBER 1942
AND SUBSEQUENT OPERATIONS
ALLIED AIRBORNE LANDINGS
AIRFIELDS

MILES 0 — 300
KILOMETRES 0 — 400

HEIGHT IN FEET
OVER 7000
5000-7000
1000-5000
UNDER 1000

Above: a map of the Torch landings and the German reaction.
Right: GIs wade ashore at Algiers in November 1942.
Below right: naval pilots are briefed for Torch aboard USS *Ranger*.

strike in three separate locations. The Western Task Force was strictly an American naval and ground operation and would sail directly from the United States. Eastern Task Force was a composite British and American operation, from which the British First Army would deploy into Tunisia while the American forces secured their immediate invasion areas.

Western Task Force, commanded by Major General George Patton, was to attack Morocco with the main effort centred around Casablanca. Center Task Force, commanded by Major General Lloyd Fredendall, would land in Algeria and concentrate its drive on Oran. Eastern Task Force, under the overall command of Major General Charles W Ryder, was to seize Algiers then swing east into Tunisia. Each of the task forces would work independently of the others. Even their landing times were different, as determined by the local tides. The objectives of the invasion forces were much the same. Each had a major city which was to be seized as rapidly as possible. Port facilities which could provide future disembarkation sites for supplies were to be secured. Airfields were to be taken quickly to provide bases for RAF and USAAF support aircraft waiting in Gibralter. Naval support for the landings was to be provided by both the Royal Navy and US Navy.

Operation Torch got underway on 8 November 1942. When elements of Patton's Western Task Force landed between 0400 and 0600 hours they were surprised by the reception afforded them. American troops had been told that pro-Allied officers in Morocco would seize control and give clearance for the landings. Patton and his staff were given a less optimistic account of the situation, but they would not know the actual state of affairs until the men hit the beaches. As Western Task Force landing craft approached the shore, loud speakers were employed to tell the French who they were and not to fire. These pleas for cooperation fell on deaf ears as the veteran French colonial troops who occupied Patton's three landing sites gave the staunchest resistance of the entire operation. Major General Ernest Harmon, whose force consisted of elements of the 9th Division and 2nd Armored Division, established a beachhead at the city of Safi by 1015 hours then spent the remainder of the day landing tanks and supplies for the second stage of his attack. Harmon's forces had suffered casualties not only from French ground troops but also from French aircraft operating from Marrakech, which was Harmon's ultimate objective. The following day invasion support aircraft destroyed the French aircraft at Marrakech and Harmon's forces moved southeast toward the city and airfield. On 10 November Harmon realized that French resistance in his area had ceased and sent units toward Casablanca to aid the American effort there.

As Harmon's troops were engaged, Patton's other two landings were in progress. As the 3rd Infantry Division landed at Fedala northeast of Casablanca, they were met by a bombardment from French shore batteries. These batteries were soon silenced by naval gunfire and the primary difficulty of the division was confusion caused by landing at the wrong beach areas. On that same day French vessels from Casablanca engaged American warships in a brief action which resulted in heavy French losses.

On 9 and 10 November units of the 9th Infantry Division under General Truscott took Port Lyautey and its airfield after bitter fighting. Also on those days Harmon's 3rd Division reconsolidated, moving toward Casablanca. At 0700 hours on 11 November Patton accepted the surrender of French forces in the area, who had been ordered to cease resistance.

Five days before Patton's initial landings the vessels carrying the other two task forces moved through the Straits of Gibralter. The convoys were immediately noted by German Intelligence but the North African invasion had been kept so secret that it was assumed the Allies were destined for either Malta, Tripoli or Suez. The Luftwaffe flew missions against the convoy but little damage was done. The invasion fleet moved into position and at 0100 hours 8 November Fredendall's Center Task Force began landing. Although sporadic resistance was met the landing was accomplished with relative ease. US Rangers swiftly neutralized the coastal batteries at Arzeu and by noon elements of the 1st Infantry Division secured that city and Les Andalouses. Two armor units were also landed, one at Arzeu and the other at Cape Figalo. These units were to swing in an enveloping maneuver to seize the airfields at Lourmel and Tafaraqui. Once this was accomplished they would proceed toward Oran to capture La Senia and the minor airfield there.

Also on that morning at 0300 hours two small naval cutters with accompanying landing forces attempted to surprise the harbor defenses at Oran. French resistance there was so intense that the assault took heavy losses and was forced to surrender. Accompanying airborne assaults were targeted for Tafaraqui, but failed initially when the paratroopers were dropped more than fifteen miles west of the city.

On 9 November French troops attempted a counterattack which was effectively repulsed by the Americans. It was not long before the American units achieved their objectives and by nightfall Oran was surrounded. By noon on 10 November French resistance in the area collapsed and the French troops surrendered.

The Eastern Task Force, whose objective was Algiers, met with the least resistance, aided by pro-Allied French officers and troops who had temporarily seized control, but they held out only until 1900 hours that evening. Admiral Jean Darlan, commander of French forces in Algeria, was taken into protective custody, negotiating an end to hostilities.

With the French pacified, British forces in Algiers turned their attention to Tunisia. On 11 and 12 November elements of the British 78th Division moved east landing at the towns of Bougie and Djidjelli. On 12 November units of the British 1st Airborne Division and 6 Commando landed unopposed at Bône to secure its airfield. The British were preparing to advance into Tunisia as behind the scenes activities of great importance were taking place. AFHQ Deputy Commander Major General Mark W Clark had entered into negotiations with Admiral Darlan not only for a ceasefire but to request French combat support in North Africa. Clark asked that French forces transfer their command to the Allies staff, though he promised that they would fight in their own units with French officers. In Europe equally important measures were being taken as the invasion progressed. Although Marshal Pétain had sought desperately to maintain the integrity of Vichy France Hitler was now convinced that the Vichy government could not stabilize the situation or control its forces beyond French borders. Hitler ordered German and Italian troops into southern France to bolster the Vichy government and to act as a deterrent against an Allied invasion of Europe through that region. At the same time Italian troops were ordered to occupy Corsica. As French forces in Africa joined the Allies it was evident that Hitler considered Vichy France as an increasingly troublesome liability.

On 12 November Darlan was stripped of his command authority by the Vichy government. It mattered little as the situation was no longer in his hands. The sympathies of most French troops lay with the Allies. They had resisted the invasion only because professional pride demanded that they follow orders, but, given justifiable cause for hope by the Allied invasion and Montgomery's recent victory over Rommel at El Alamein, French forces shifted their allegiance to the Allied Command. In Tunisia French General Barré, although ordered to resist by the Vichy government, began moving his forces west into the mountains of Tunisia to create a buffer zone between himself and the occupying Axis army. Fortunately for Barré the German commander was fully occupied with the threat posed by the Allied advance. On 17 November, under orders from Darlan who was now considered French High Commissioner in North Africa, Barré moved his forces to rendezvous with British columns as they approached the Tunisian frontier.

The acceptance of Darlan as the commander of French forces was done for expediency and was not without its problems. French military personnel who had joined the Allies after the Battle of France and who saw General Charles De Gaulle as the commander of Free French considered Darlan a collaborator who changed his position to suit his own purposes, not the best interest of France.

As the Allied effort moved toward Tunisia it became apparent that a race was underway. Axis forces in North Africa were in retreat. Tunisia, primarily the region of the port city Tunis, would be the most advantageous point for a last active defense and the most logical point for the evacuation of Axis forces from Africa to Sicily should the need arise. The situation did not favor the Allies. The western part of Tunisia through which they approached was rough mountainous terrain which gave limited access and excellent defensive positions to the enemy. German and Italian forces moving into the country from the east had relatively easy access. Nor was the Axis command taking risks with troop strength. Experienced reinforcements from the 10th Panzer Division and 334th Infantry Division were sent to bolster the defense. The elite Hermann Goering Panzer Division was also expected to add its weight.

On 18 November the British command sent a mobile task force to reinforce British and French forces in western Tunisia. This force would become the British First Army and the first American units, elements of the 1st Armored Division, would move to combine with the British 6th Armored Division. A rapid advance to Tunis was intended for late November. The British commander believed this maneuver to be the most productive. Allied and Axis forces were concentrated in the northern half of the country just opposite Tunis, leaving the southern sector relatively quiet.

As the last week of November arrived German troops had succeeded in cancelling the gains made by Allied forces in the area. Winter rains hampered the movement of supplies and materiel but the greatest problem had been the Luftwaffe, which could strike easily at the Allied positions, maintaining a superiority that would take some time for the Allies to nullify.

December saw German positions strengthening daily as General von Arnim took command of Axis forces in Tunisia and the newly formed Fifth Panzer Army. Although Eisenhower ordered First Army commander General Anderson to continue the pressure he realized that until the Allies established forward air bases little change could be expected. This fact was emphasized later in December as yet another attempt was made by Allied forces to break through to Tunis. By the end of December the race to Tunis was over. Axis forces had secured the area. Eisenhower realized that a substantial, concerted effort would have to be made to drive the enemy out of the country.

With the coming of the New Year Anderson's First Army, reinforced by troops from Morocco, swung into central Tunisia where the weather hampered mobility less. Montgomery's Eighth Army, driving the remnants of Rommel's Afrika Korps back from the east, was not destined to reach Tunisia until late February. Immediate plans for the First Army were cancelled and American and British troops took a defensive posture, making only probing attacks to search for weaknesses in the German lines. Arnim continued the pressure, making strikes against French positions in retaliation for their defection to the Allied camp. American units of the 1st and 34th Divisions were deployed to reinforce and take primary responsibility for the French sectors.

By mid-February the advantage swung more fully in German favor as the Afrika Korps prepared to link with von Arnim's Fifth Panzer Army. Immediately upon his arrival Rommel prepared a strategy for a German offensive. His plan was simple. The Fifth Panzer Army would move to seize an area known as Sidi Bou Zid while the Afrika Korps moved to Gafsa. The attacks would be directed against American sectors as Rommel believed the less experienced Americans would be the most easy prey. On 14 February 1943 the offensive began. Although the American units were expecting activity on the line they were not properly established to conduct a viable defense. Units were unable to offer support to one another and the best of the American forces, the 1st Armored Division was still attached to the French XIX Corps at Maktar. The German attack devastated the American sector throwing the entire line into confusion. On 15 February the Americans attempted to counterattack with armor but the column was virtually destroyed by veteran Afrika Korps *Panzer* forces. Later that day the British released the remaining units of the American 1st Armored Division. In spite of the odds the American defenses held at three crucial points; at Sbeitla where the remnants of the 1st Armored Division were concentrated, at Kasserine and Fériana.

On 16 February the *Panzers* renewed their attacks at Sbeitla but in the face of overwhelming odds the Americans continued to hold. The following day a

Above: a US Ranger battalion marches over difficult terrain in Tunisia, January 1943.
Right: an American camp set up at Bizerta after the German surrender in North Africa.

35

calm evacuation of the area was conducted. As the 1st Armored Division was withdrawing sections of the 10th Panzer Division moved toward Kasserine while Rommel, having taken Fériana, maneuvered to rendezvous with the 10th Panzers. The situation appeared lost and American forces prepared a hasty withdrawal. That withdrawal was given an opportunity for execution as disagreement between von Arnim and Rommel delayed the German advance by one day.

On 19 February Rommel was granted supreme command of all armored forces in the region. He ordered an immediate advance through the Kasserine Pass and although American troops offered staunch resistance they were soon outflanked and forced to fall back. Over the next two days Rommel continued to put pressure on American forces blocking the path to his main objective, Tebéssa. American resistance had given the British time to establish a strong defensive line north of the Kasserine Pass near Thala. Rommel was forced to admit that his drive had lost both initiative and momentum. He withdrew from the area unmolested but the rift between himself and von Arnim had caused a critical delay which would ultimately cost the Axis Powers North Africa.

As Rommel reconsolidated the Allies realized they must reevaluate their position in Tunisia. American and British forces were scattered throughout the north central area. The 18th Army Group Commander in direct charge of the North Africa operations, British General Harold Alexander, decided that the situation must wait for the arrival of General Montgomery's Eighth Army. Only through the combined efforts of Anderson's First Army and Montgomery's Eighth could the balance weigh in Allied favor. The Americans had fought bravely but their inexperience led them to rash, unpredictable reactions which jeopardized the operations. The realization of the need for further training was a major concern. Thus II Corps, which consisted of the 1st, 9th and 34th Infantry Divisions and the 1st Armored Division, was placed under General Patton's command for limited involvement in the impending operations. Patton's primary function would be to maneuver to the southernmost front, drawing off German troops from Montgomery's drive to Mareth. Patton was also to capture Gafsa as a supply point and conduct reconnaissance at Maknassy. Patton was displeased with this arrangement. He wanted to advance to Sfax, thus trapping the German First Army between himself and Montgomery, but Alexander stood firm refusing Patton any margin in his precise orders. The Americans would have to be tested further before being given a primary offensive role again. Although Patton must grudgingly have realized the fundamental truth of Alexander's position the situation angered him and would rancor throughout the war. To some extent Patton's position was equally justified. Although

Above: General Omar Bradley relieved Patton of the command of the US II Corps in North Africa and led the attack on Bizerta.

American units had not excelled in Tunisia the experience gained in late February had taken them from green recruits to combat veterans. Patton firmly believed that the best place to train men was to take them into the fray where victory meant survival.

On 20 March Montgomery swung his forces to engage the German southernmost flank. After three days of slow progress he was driven back by a German counterattack. On 26 March he launched yet another assault, which, though more successful than the first, did not manage to encircle or capture the German and Italian defenders. While Montgomery's offensive was in progress Patton decided that the most effective way to draw German forces away would be to attack. He ordered an advance into the plains area by attacking near El Guettar and Maknassy. On 23 March the 1st Armored Division held the Germans at bay while the 9th and 34th Divisions advanced. Although little initial progress was made Patton succeeded in turning a corner which would place Allied troops within reach of the coastal plains.

By 6 April Montgomery had pushed through the German lines and on the following day Patton's II Corps rendezvoused with the Eighth Army north of El Hamma. Although the event produced a lift in Allied morale the maneuver had failed to entrap a sizeable number of enemy troops. On 8 April the British First

Above: a group of dejected Axis troops made prisoners of war during the fighting in Tunisia.

Army took temporary command of the 34th Division to renew attacks on Fondouk at the center of the front. Again little progress was initially made but the combined attacks on the Axis defensive line, particularly on the southern flank, weakened the German position and enabled the Fondouk assault to breach the line. By 12 April elements of Anderson's First Army and the 34th Division joined Montgomery's forces near Kairouan. The entire southern region of Tunisia had been secured. The following day British troops pursued their advantage pushing the German army back to the northern third of the country near Tunis.

With the gains he had made in the south and the effectiveness of his support for Montgomery, Patton applied for a more active role in the final offensives. Alexander reluctantly gave approval for the II Corps' transfer from the south to the northern sector with responsibility for the protection of the Allied left flank. The day before the transfer was approved the II Corps command changed. Major General Omar N Bradley rose to that command freeing Patton to return to Morocco to oversee troop training for the anticipated invasion of Sicily. Alexander's decision was obviously influenced by General Eisenhower. Eisenhower took the position that eventually the greatest burden of war would fall to American forces, particularly for the invasion of Europe. As such American troops and perhaps more importantly American field com-

manders, would need time and experience to meet the challenge ahead. Whatever the deciding factor, American troops would be an integral part of the final Tunis offensive.

Alexander's strategy for the offensive was put into operation. Anderson's First Army reinforced by an armored division from Montgomery's command would make the primary assault. Anderson's objective would be to thrust through the central Axis defense then proceed directly northeast to Tunis. On the southern flank Montgomery's army and the 19th French Corps would undertake a secondary assault. Bradley's II Corps would provide a diversion in the north, thus immobilizing the Axis flanks. The Allied air effort in North Africa had by this time neutralized the Luftwaffe and would support the offensive by applying pressure to the Axis rear areas, cutting off their retreat to Tunis. Allied morale was further heightened by the removal of the 'Desert Fox' Rommel from the scene. Failing health had forced him to return to Europe and the less 'frightening' von Arnim took over his command.

When the offensive began on 3 May 1943 the Americans would prove Alexander's fears unfounded. Although the opposition they faced was not as strong as that on other sectors the Americans made the largest gains. By the end of the month all four American divisions had acquitted themselves well, taking each of their objectives in rapid succession and driving off every enemy counterattack launched against them. On 3 May the 1st Armored Division took Mateur and was prepared to cut off any enemy forces in its quadrant. As the British thrusts advanced Bradley never allowed his corps to fall behind. With each day American troops gained confidence and respect as they followed on the heels of the Axis withdrawal. The port city of Bizerte fell to the 9th Infantry Division on 7 May. Two days later armored elements broke through to capture Protville.

The Axis defenses were put to flight by 7 May and Anderson's army captured Tunis, but not before the more elite units such as the Hermann Goering Division had escaped by sea. From 9 to 13 May Allied forces swept across Tunisia. On 13 May the First Italian Army surrendered to Montgomery. In all the Allies captured nearly 250,000 enemy troops during those final days, 20 percent of whom were prisoners of Bradley's corps.

For the Americans Tunisia had been an important training ground which demonstrated their ability to perform as expected in the worst possible conditions. Rommel himself had paid the American troops a tribute after he dealt them their worst defeat at Kasserine. He said, 'they may be inexperienced and ignorant of mechanized tactics but they learn quickly.' North Africa had not only given the Allies their first true victory but had given the American command and troops a vital opportunity to learn their lessons.

5 THE SOFT UNDERBELLY?

As the battles for North Africa were being fought Churchill and Roosevelt met at Casablanca to formulate strategies for the invasion of Europe. The Casablanca Conference would determine the directions to be taken, but the United States was not in a firm position for bargaining at the time. Although America had been at war for one year full mobilization had not yet been achieved. American involvement in North Africa was perceived as merely providing support to the British operation. The bulk of men and ships had been supplied by Britain and, although this was actually the last time that Britain would hold the weight of power, it was a crucial balance.

Although Marshall agreed with Churchill's European invasion schemes, the Chief of Staff continued to oppose the Mediterranean concept. The British perspective recognized concerns about which the Americans were thought to be naive. First, North Africa was the only location where British troops were truly in contention. A victory there would not only provide morale incentive but would strengthen Churchill's political position. Rommel's 'wizardry' had kept the British from achieving unaided victory in Africa. At Casablanca Churchill proposed an invasion of the 'soft underbelly' of Europe. Allied troops were already in the Mediterranean and an attack on Italy would be the next logical step to Europe. Italian troops had never demonstrated a keen combat ability and were considered only reasonable troops even when reinforced by German soldiers. An invasion of Italy would produce one of two results. Either Hitler would have to pull troops from other areas of Europe to reinforce Italy or he would have to let his Axis ally fall, establishing a German defensive line elsewhere. Either alternative would prove costly for Germany. If Hitler reinforced his ally it would cause manpower problems in Europe, but if he let Italy fall the Allies would have a great victory over one of the three Axis Powers.

Churchill's strategy made sense to Roosevelt who

overruled American objections. It was decided that the offensive against southern Europe would be undertaken in two phases. The first, Operation Husky, called for an Allied invasion of Sicily. Success in Sicily would most likely result in an invasion of southern Italy, though a landing in southern France was not ruled out at Casablanca. The Soviet Union had been calling for the Allies to establish a second front in Europe and Roosevelt believed the Mediterranean operations would also serve to appease Stalin. It was also after Casablanca that FDR called for the unconditional surrender of the three Axis Powers. This position was taken to illustrate to occupied peoples that no deals or secret agreements were being made that sacrificed their nations for peace. The Casablanca Conference also dealt with strategic bombing, security of the open seas, Allied strategies in the Far East and the possibility of bringing Turkey into the Allied effort. French leaders were brought into the Allied discussions and for the first time displayed a small measure of solidarity. General De Gaulle strove to act as the leader of the French though Roosevelt and Churchill did not fully recognize him as such and rifts in the French command continued.

At the conference Eisenhower was directed to begin preparations for Operation Husky, to be implemented in July 1943. Although the Americans continued to hope for a cross-Channel invasion of France in 1943 the prospects grew dim as the year progressed. When it became obvious that the invasion of France was not immediately forthcoming Admiral King began to complain that the armada lying idle in Britain could be put to far better use in the Pacific. King would eventually win and this would later be reflected in the curious entourage of vessels used for D-Day.

Later that year at the Trident Conference Churchill stressed the point that the Sicily invasion was not an end in itself, but that Italy would be invaded by troops already in the Mediterranean theater and Allied troops dispatched from Britain. Italy must be eliminated and Sicily was an essential stepping stone to that end. It was with this in mind that the plans for Operation Husky were designed. All usable ports were to be seized for support of Allied operations. Second and equally important was the rapid capture of airfields which could provide bases for close support aircraft. Original plans called for two separate invasions and naval diversionary action. The British Eighth Army, still under Montgomery's command, was to land on the southeast coast of Sicily below Syracuse while the American Seventh Army commanded by General Patton struck selected beaches in southwest Sicily near Licata. The American invasion was to land two to five days prior to the British assault which was to surprise the enemy as it maneuvered to counter Patton's threat. Montgomery naturally objected to this plan and upon further study Eisenhower decided that the logistics involved in distinctly different

Below: a laden LCT passes a row of transports during the landings in Sicily, Operation Husky, which involved some 1200 transports and 2000 landing craft.

attacks plus the inadequate opportunity to seize airfields made the plan impractical. The landings would be simultaneous.

Naval diversions in the area fooled only Hitler himself, who ordered the immediate reinforcement of Corsica, Sardinia and Greece. These diversions were the responsibility of Admiral Bertram Ramsay, who commanded Allies naval invasion operations. Ramsay was one of the most competent Allied naval officers whose reputation had been heightened by his role in the successful evacuation of British forces at Dunkirk.

The Allied convoys left North Africa on 9 July. Heavy seas and strong winds threatened to turn the invasion fleets back, but shortly after midnight the winds moderated and by 0230 hours on 10 July the invasion was back on schedule. Although the rough waters were considered by many as an omen of disaster they would in fact prove to be a blessing. The Sicily defenders were taken by surprise, having considered the sea too treacherous for Allied vessels to challenge. As the beaches were reached special landing craft were used to put the troops on the beaches. Tanks, which would prove extremely valuable in the days to come, were landed safely. Encountering virtually no resistance eight divisions from some 1000 ships created a beachhead front more than 100 miles wide. The initial invasion was an overwhelming success. By nightfall the assault divisions had secured their areas and troops and supplies were pouring ashore.

Although Allied naval operations were a great success, airborne support operations were not. The winds had blown aircraft off course, scattering paratroopers and gliders over the southern area of Sicily. One airborne unit, the US 505th Paratroop Regiment, managed to seize the high ground at Vittoria and Ragusa. Once organized the regiment established road blocks and repulsed all enemy movement and counterattacks. Axis forces could easily have overwhelmed the regiment, but the determined American action had convinced them that an extremely large Allied force was present. The British 1st Parachute Division also concentrated to hold a bridgehead until the British ground advance could reach them. However on 11 July the luck granted the airborne forces apparently ran out. The US 504th Regiment, dropped in to reinforce the ground troops were mistaken by Allied naval and shore batteries for a German counterattack and the regiment was virtually destroyed by antiaircraft fire. On 13 July British paratroopers suffered a similar fate when being dropped in to reinforce their own lines. The Allied Command immediately suspended airborne operations for the time being.

Once established ashore the two armies turned their attention to the primary objective, the capture of the port city Messina. The British Eighth Army was to proceed directly north along the coastal road for an

assault from the south. Although this was the shortest route it was also the most difficult. Half way to their objective, near Catania, the terrain became more difficult. Mount Etna and the surrounding highlands would certainly slow the British advance and give added advantage to enemy defenders. Patton's Seventh Army was to advance west along the shoreline capturing the coastal port cities then turning north to seize Palermo. From there those forces would move along the northern coast to join Montgomery's assault on Messina. Patton had much farther to travel but his operations were designed to draw Axis forces away from the main British advance.

A critical day for the Americans was 11 July, when German armored units took positions above the beachhead at Gela and launched an attack to drive the Americans back into the sea. Here in twenty-four hours the Seventh Army would suffer more casualties than it would sustain throughout the rest of the Sicily campaign. American forward positions which had not yet received armor or antitank support were forced to fall back. Though taken by surprise their lines bent but did not break. Through the combined efforts of naval gunfire, artillery, tanks and dogged infantry fighting the ground was held. American combat abilities would never again be questioned, by either side.

Unknown to the Allied Command the results at

Far left: a US reconnaissance
patrol clears snipers from the
streets of Messina.
Left: a military policeman
checks the papers of a German
POW captured in Sicily.
Below: a US tank pursues
retreating German troops
through a Sicilian village.

Gela forced Field Marshal Albert Kesselring, supreme German commander in the region, to accept that Sicily was a lost cause and concentrate his army at Messina for easy evacuation to the mainland of Italy. Yet as German forces began to pull out resistance in Sicily was maintained. Between 12 and 15 July Allied forces began to link, forming a continuous line from Augusta on the east coast to just south of Porto Empedocle. Sporadic resistance did not prevent the Allies from seizing and putting into operation several crucial airfields in Sicily. On 15 July Alexander issued directives on the methods for the securing of Sicily. Montgomery's army was to advance on either side of Mount Etna and was to have the glory of capturing Messina. Patton was to continue his advance on Palermo, while protecting Montgomery's rear and performing mop up operations. Patton was again displeased with his assignment, accusing Montgomery and Alexander of putting too much emphasis on the British effort. Eisenhower had repeatedly emphasized the need for cooperation and Patton knew he would get no support from that quarter. He could however extend his operations without actually violating orders.

Alexander had told Patton what he must do but had not given Patton a precise timetable. For Patton the extension of his objective might mean more ground to cover but he considered a race to Messina to be on. Shifting two divisions to Bradley's command, which was to move directly across the island to the north coast to comply with orders to protect Montgomery's rear area, Patton took the remainder of the Seventh Army and struck out to capture western Sicily. In an advance reminiscent of Jackson's Shenandoah Valley Campaign Patton swept across Sicily, traveling more than 100 miles in less than 96 hours. On 23 July Patton and the 2nd Armored Division entered Palermo in triumph. He then turned the 1st, 3rd and 45th Divisions east. Bradley's troops, struggling to keep pace with the British in the rugged terrain, took the brunt of fighting. Bradley's men were soon facing veteran German units, including sections of the 1st Parachute Division and the Hermann Goering Division.

Patton's success had been obvious early in his initial advance and before he even reached Palermo Alexander recognized the momentum that his attack was building. Montgomery's progress had been slow and reluctant so Alexander gave Patton authorization to do anything necessary to take Messina. Twice in his eastern advance Patton called on the navy to land his troops beyond German defenses to keep the drive rolling. Ironically his drive had put such pressure on the Axis defenders that they were drawn away from Montgomery's forces and the Eighth Army began to gain momentum. It would be only a matter of days before one army or the other reached Messina.

41

On 17 August, just hours ahead of the British columns American troops captured Messina. The rivalry which had begun in North Africa and had been so obvious in Sicily was big news on the home fronts. In many cases reports lost sight of the victory which had been achieved, dwelling on the ramifications of the Patton-Montgomery rivalry. The initial elation over the liberation of Sicily was dampened by the knowledge that Kesselring had successfully evacuated 40,000 German and 70,000 Italian troops and all their equipment between 3 and 17 August. However the implications of the conquest of Sicily and the repercussions they caused in Italy were decisive. Three days after Patton took Palermo, Mussolini was ousted by the Fascist Grand Council by a vote of no confidence. The armed forces of Italy were given over to King Victor Emmanuel and Marshal Pietro Badoglio became Prime Minister. The first of the Axis dictators had been deposed.

The more important result of the Sicily success was

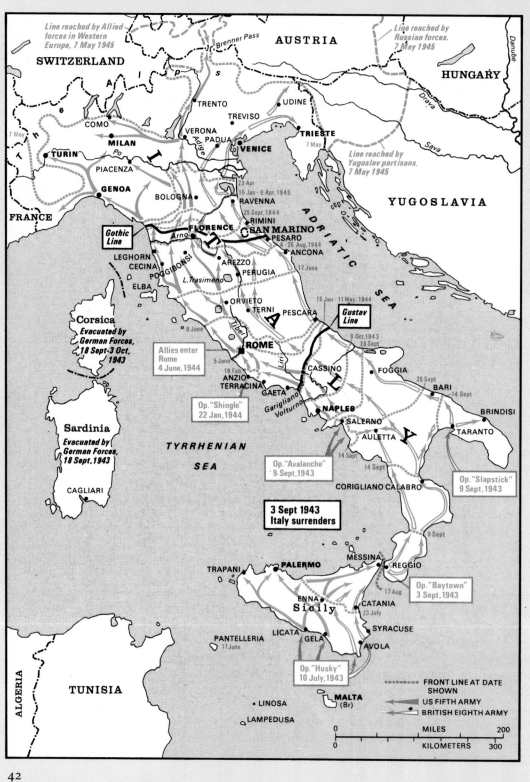

Left: a map showing Allied operations in Italy from the Sicily landings until the end of World War II in Europe. Above: the Italian surrender is announced aboard a troopship, but the jubilation was premature as much hard fighting in Italy lay ahead. Above right: General Mark Clark (left) is pictured with Admiral Alan Kirk.

revealed after 26 August when Eisenhower confirmed his plans for the invasion of Italy at Salerno. The situation in Italy had become such that neither the people nor the government wanted to continue the war. However the German armies would not leave Italy without a fight. Although there appeared little he could do to save his country, Prime Minister Badoglio approached the Allies to negotiate a secret peace providing the Allies invaded northern Italy sparing the south from the ravages of war. The Allied com-

dence in men and materiel in 1944.

The American command began to look upon an invasion of Italy in a more favorable light as a guarantee of success in Operation Overlord, the invasion of northern France. A number of strategic objectives could be accomplished through such an invasion. The most important were the elimination of Italy from the war and the threatening of Germany's southern borders. Large quantities of Italian and German equipment would be lost to Germany

mand could not be persuaded. On 3 September Italy surrendered secretly. Whether or not these negotiations held to the guidelines established at the Casablanca Conference could not be determined. Expediency was of primary importance. In any case the Italian government moved its headquarters south and Mussolini was placed under arrest for crimes against the state. He would not long remain an Italian prisoner as German commandos rescued him a short time later.

In spite of their advantages the Allies continued to have problems with conflicting American and British strategic objectives. The British with traditional Mediterranean interests wanted either an invasion of Italy or the Balkans. US Chief of Staff Marshall was still pressing for an invasion of France. He personally considered the Mediterranean operations a waste of American resources and was finding it increasingly difficult to convince Pacific commanders that the fighting in Europe was not drawing equipment or supplies from the war against Japan. Finally in August 1943 at the Quadrant Conference the Combined Chiefs of Staff set a date for the invasion of western Europe. The operation would be a combined British-American venture which would take prece-

through the surrender and occupation of Italy. Furthermore Italian troop garrisons in southern France and the Balkans would immediately be lost to Germany forcing the Reich to supplement these areas by relocating troops from other European fronts. Yet another crucial factor was the effect of Italian occupation on the air war. Airfields in Italy would give Allied bombers more easy access to the secluded regions to which Germany's industries had been dispersed. The possibility of 'shuttle' missions flying from Britain, across Europe to Italy to rearm and refuel for return missions was also tempting. Not least in importance was the boost to morale which would be gained by the defeat and occupation of one Axis Power. It was bound to put new energy into the Allied war effort.

In July Lieutenant General Mark Clark, commander of the US Fifth Army, whose task it was to initiate the attack at Salerno, prepared his invasion plans and submitted them for approval. His plan called for intense air strikes and a diversionary naval assault in the Gulf of Gaeta, north of the actual invasion zone. The British Eighth Army was to initiate a secondary front across the Straits from Messina at the 'toe' of Italy. It was hoped that this

43

attack would draw German attention from the actual invasion site. Other elements of the Eighth Army were to cross the Ionian Sea to set a diversionary assault against Taranto. When the Fifth Army attacked at Salerno south of Naples it was intended that the combined operations would trap and destroy the German defenders.

On 3 September, as the Italian surrender was secretly negotiated, two divisions of the Eighth Army crossed the straits from Messina meeting minimal resistance. For the next four days vessels carrying the main invasion force assembled at sea. On 8 September they sailed into the Gulf of Salerno for their assault on 9 September. On the morning of 9 September the British 1st Paratroop Division made an amphibious assault on the Italian naval base at Taranto.

When Italy officially announced its surrender on 8 September Kesselring was prepared. He ordered all Italian units disarmed and all troops imprisoned. Fighting broke out between German and Italian troops in Rome. The Italian fleet made a dash to the safety of Malta harassed the entire way by the Luftwaffe. The Allies had hoped that the announcement of Italy's surrender just prior to the invasion would throw the German command and forces into confusion. There was such confidence in the ensuing

civil unrest and weakness of the German position in Italy that Clark anticipated only sporadic resistance, claiming that Allied troops would be in Rome before Christmas.

At 0330 hours 9 September the Fifth Army landed at Salerno. Rangers landed at Maiori unopposed and began moving inland to Nocera to bisect the main coastal road to Naples. On the Ranger's left flank British commandos landed and moved into Salerno. The Commandos and the British 46th and 56th Divisions made fairly easy landings though the divisions encountered determined opposition south of Salerno. On the southern flank the American VI Corps landed only one division, the inexperienced 36th Infantry. The division was to secure the southernmost right flank but due to some confusion in orders they were not supported by naval or air operations. Resistance in this sector was the heaviest encountered and although the 36th took heavy casualties they continued to advance, taking their primary objective Paestum and two nearby hills before nightfall. As the invasion forces struggled to advance over the next 48 hours it became obvious that German units were consolidating for a counterattack.

On 12 September that attack materialized, directed at the center of the Allied line where the American and

Left: an LCVP from the USS *James O'Hare* beaches at Salerno under German shellfire. Chicken wire has been laid over the sand to prevent vehicles sinking in.
Above: a 105mm howitzer is brought into action in support of US Rangers fighting in the hills above Naples.

British corps were linked. The American 45th Division, which landed several days earlier, and the 36th Division had been under intense pressure since their landing and took heavy casualties as the German assault ripped through their lines. The British 56th Division was also struck but managed to fall back in good order, maintaining contact with the American Divisions and preventing the German forces from breaking through to the rear beach areas. By the next day the situation had become so desperate that American artillery, usually safely in the rear, found itself on the front line. The artillerymen stood their ground firing point-blank at German assault waves. The exploits of these artillerymen have been favorably compared to their historic Napoleonic or Civil War counterparts who stood in the face of overwhelming odds. By nightfall American losses were so great that two battalions of the 82nd Airborne Division were dropped onto the beaches as reinforcements.

By 14 September it appeared as though the American lines would crumble yet they held their ground until the full weight of naval bombardment and American fighter and bomber aircraft could be brought to bear on the German troop concentration. On that same day the problems encountered by the naval task force were rectified and the British 7th Armoured Division landed to reinforce the line. The German offensive was crushed. On 15 September, although there was sporadic fighting, the battle for the beachhead was won and the Germans were withdrawing to a defensive position. The success of the operation was due not only to the staunch resistance of Allied troops but to an error of judgement made by the German command. Kesselring, who had taken command of the defense of southern Italy, did not have the support of Rommel who had been given command of German forces in northern Italy. The two men had differing opinions as to the proper defense of Italy and Rommel refused Kesselring's request for three divisions to bolster the German counterattack.

As the battle for the beaches at Salerno was raging the British Eighth Army was sweeping up from the south. On 17 September the British 5th Division made contact with American forces 40 miles south of Salerno. Allied successes forced Kesselring to adopt his defensive posture. By 1 October Naples was occupied by Allied troops and although German engineers had attempted to destroy the harbor their American counterparts had it fully operational by 6 October. By 8 October the Fifth and Eighth Armies had a line which stretched from the Volturno River on the west coast of Italy to the city of Termoli on the east coast. It was here that Kesselring had established his winter defense line. Although it was not the perfect point of defense Kesselring saw the line as one of many available to his forces to impede and inflict casualties on the Allies.

October saw German reinforcements rushed to Italy and the Balkans and the evacuation of Corsica and Sardinia. Although the strain was not initially felt these troops should have been directed to the Russian Front. As the situation became more critical troops would also be drawn to northern Italy from France. Eventually the effects of these deployments would be felt. Throughout October and November Allied forces struggled to break through the German defenses which had fallen back to the Garigliano River in the Apennines. The defense was centered around the monastery on Monte Cassino. American and British forces repeatedly assaulted this defense, known as the Gustav Line, accomplishing little but increased casualties and troop exhaustion. Not only was the Gustav Line an obstacle but the weather had created its own form of interference to Allied operations. It rained for days at a time, washing away bridges and creating a quagmire through which not even foot soldiers could move. Gains were paid for dearly as the Allied troops faced not only the German defenses but the extensive booby-trap and mining operations which had been conducted in areas through which the Fifth Army would have to pass.

As Allied movement stagnated and the German defenses became more formidable, Alexander and Churchill took special interest in the suggestion that another invasion be made behind the Gustav Line at Anzio. A landing at Anzio would place Allied troops only a few miles south of Rome. There were many strategists opposed to the concept. They argued that it would place troops too far behind enemy lines, 60 miles north of the Gustav Line. Fears were also expressed that the force landed might find it difficult to break away from the beaches and would be unable to reach the Gustav defenses rapidly enough to be of any assistance. Others believed that Kesselring would simply ignore the landings entirely. One argument in favor of the invasion which could not be ignored was the possibility it gave of severing Kesselring's lines of supply. The disruption of those lines would force the German army to abandon its defensive position and withdraw.

Before he would give final approval to the Anzio scheme Alexander ordered the Eighth Army to attempt to swing around the Gustav Line. Over the next month Allied forces assaulted the position, but the only measurable degree of success came between 5 and 15 January 1944 when the American II Corps was able to advance to the Rapido River. Part of this attack force included the 100th Battalion of the First Special Service Force Brigade, comprised of Japanese Americans. The appearance of these men caused great confusion in the German ranks as they could not understand what the Japanese were doing in Italy fighting for the Allies. This battalion would distinguish itself through the war in Europe and on this occasion

Left: a machine gunner of the 143rd Infantry Division outside Giugliano on the Gothic Line.

many of its members sacrificed their lives to save a group of American soldiers trapped by a German encirclement. As the assault slowly ground to a halt the idea of landings behind Kesselring's lines resurfaced.

A coordinated plan of attack was formulated. The British X Corps of Clark's Fifth Army would make probing attacks on the lower Garigliano River in an effort to pull the German defenders out of position. It would then be up to the US II Corps to advance in the Liri Valley toward Frosinone while French units attached to the Fifth Army maneuvered to the mountains near Monte Cassino. During these operations the VI Corps under the command of American Major General John P Lucas would make an amphibious landing in the Anzio-Nettuno region. Once ashore their objective was the Alban Hills just south of Rome to sever Kesselring's supply lines. These actions, coupled with sustained pressure on the

German left flank by the Eighth Army would force Kesselring to retreat. The Allied commanders also realized that once Kesselring's forces had been dislodged from the Gustav Line there were no truly defensible positions between there and Rome itself.

On 21 January the amphibious assault force sailed from Naples, landing at their beaches at 0200 hours. Although German Intelligence had warned of the possibility of such an assault the defenders were taken by surprise and Lucas landed virtually unopposed. Having successfully landed his forces without difficulty Lucas then made a fatal error. Rather than pursue his objective immediately he paused for nearly one week to consolidate his forces, equipment and supplies. Had he advanced immediately German defenses were so thin that he might have walked to Rome unchallenged and taken his objectives by noon of 22 January. Lucas' actions have often been criticized as resulting in the near destruction of the VI Corps by

Above: troops of the US Fifth Army fight their way into Santa Maria east of Pisa.

the German counterattack. It will never be known whether a rapid advance would have been successful. On 30 January as Lucas prepared to move inland Kesselring struck first. The German troops were on the verge of handing the Americans their worst defeat since the Kasserine Pass. As Lucas struggled against the punishment being delivered, an American Ranger battalion of 800 men attempted to reach out and seize Cisterna at the foot of the Alban Hills. Only six of those Rangers would escape death or capture. The prisoners of this battalion would be marched through the streets of Rome in a demonstration of German military superiority. On 16 February the German forces renewed their offensive and nearly drove the Anzio invasion force back into the sea. Although the attack was repulsed the invasion was considered a disaster. Lucas was removed from command to be replaced by Major General Lucian Truscott.

At the Gustav Line Clark prepared a series of attacks along the river at Monte Cassino. He and General Juin's Free French forces tried desperately to breach the defenses but were repulsed, though the British 10th Division managed to cross the Garigliano River. The failure of this primary effort created even more frustration in the Allied camps. The battle around Monte Cassino was taking an intolerable toll. The ancient monastery which overlooked the valley and river was obviously the best possible position and the Allied commanders were convinced that the Germans had established defenses and artillery observation posts in the monastery. Although the use of such religious shrines as that at Monte Cassino, where the Benedictine Order had begun, was against the rules of warfare, it was assumed that Kesselring's forces were ignoring this sanction. As a result the Allies decided to reduce the monastery to rubble. In fact though the German paratroopers were on Monte Cassino they had observed the code. Kesselring had given strict orders that the monastery was not to be violated. The Allies would realize later, after it was too late, that they had made an irrevocable mistake. On 15 February Allied bombers destroyed the monastery. It was a grave tactical blunder. Not only had they failed to eliminate the German artillery sites, which were carefully camouflaged elsewhere in the mountains, but they had given the Germans just cause to convert the rubble into a viable defense. General Clark would regret the destruction not only for the lives wasted dislodging German troops from the rubble, but because he had sanctioned the destruction of a building that had withstood the ravages of time.

The following day the American 34th Division and New Zealand forces attacked what they believed was a weakened German position only to find that the Gustav Line was indeed impregnable. Clark conferred with Alexander and it was decided that a reevaluation of the situation was in order. Montgomery had been recalled to England to assist in the planning for the invasion of northern France and General Oliver Leese was now in command of the Eighth Army. It was decided that a portion of that army would join the front at the monastery. After careful reconsolidation the Allied offensive was in readiness. On 11 May 1944 two divisions of the Eighth Army pushed across the Rapido River with a Polish Corps and two divisions of Moroccans. It was not until a week later that Polish troops entered the monastery from the north after a bitter hand-to-hand battle. This accomplished the British and American X and II Corps advanced through the Liri Valley and along the coastal plains against strong opposition. Kesselring now saw his Gustav Line cracked and, although his troops offered staunch resistance, by 23 May he was forced to withdraw northwest of Rome. On that same day six Allied divisions raced up the coast to relieve the Anzio beachhead defense.

The fall from that point on was rapid. On 4 June

Above: in April 1945 the former Italian dictator Mussolini was captured and executed by Italian partisans. His body was hung in the Piazzo Loretto in Milan.

American soldiers entered Rome after it had been declared an open city. Although it appeared that the Americans had finally caught the German Tenth Army, Clark shifted his strength to Rome and Anzio, letting Kesselring escape. American troops were in Rome six months later than the time schedule had demanded and only two days before the Normandy Invasion, but operations in Italy were by no means ended. Kesselring had established a new defense, the Gothic Line, which extended from Pisa in the northeast to Rimini on the Adriatic Sea. In advance of that primary defense he established a secondary line along the Arno River to include Florence and the area between the Allies and Rimini. This advanced line was intended to slow the Allied advance and give the defenses on the Gothic Line time to be strengthened. Here the two sides would remain throughout the winter of 1944–45 with Kesselring again in the mountains and the weather hampering Allied operations.

During that time Alexander took charge of the seven Allied divisions that were to invade southern France in conjunction with the Normandy Invasion and Clark succeeded Alexander as Commander of 15th Army Group. Allied troops throughout the Mediterranean found their numbers and resources greatly reduced as attention and priorities were focused on Western Europe. It would not be until April 1945 that Truscott's Fifth Army would force the Germans out of the hills, into the Po Valley and across the river to Austria. The British Eighth Army would accelerate the retreat but the war was practically over. Kesselring had been recalled to Germany to establish a home defense and with German resources shifted to Germany resistance in Italy was swiftly crushed.

April also saw the death of Benito Mussolini. He had since his rescue from an Italian prison been the head of a German puppet government in northern Italy. He lived the life of a captive in exile, owing his life to German protection. When Truscott's forces broke through the lines at the Po Valley the German army in retreat left Mussolini behind at the mercy of the Italian government established by the Allies. Before he could be taken into custody he was caught and killed by members of the Italian Communist partisans of the Volunteer Freedom Corps on 28 April 1945. The following day his body along with those of his mistress Claretta Petacci and two other Fascist leaders was displayed, hung by their heels, in Milan. The Italian people mutilated the bodies in a display of bitter hatred for their former leader. He had promised them so much and had given them only the destruction of war.

It had taken the Allies one year and ten months to conquer Sicily and Italy. The soft underbelly of Europe had proven to be a 'tough old gut.' Italy would be the last of the British dominated fronts as Alexander continued to limit the American role in the Mediterranean in spite of Clark's attempts to change that situation. The Mediterranean campaign had served its purpose. It could never in itself have won the war but its contribution to the fall of the Third Reich had been considerable.

6 OVERLORD

From the entrance of the United States into the war with Germany and Italy the liberation of occupied Europe had been an underlying and deciding factor in American policymaking. The proposal set forth by Marshall to accomplish that goal called for a concentration of men, materiel, ships and aircraft in Britain for an invasion across the English Channel. Such an invasion would strain the German war machine to the limits as it attempted to wage total war on both its eastern and western borders. In 1942 thoughts of an European invasion were quickly put aside. The United States was simply not prepared for such an undertaking. Operation Torch in North Africa was given priority with the hope that in 1943 the situation would have stabilized sufficiently to allow for consideration of a European venture. Again the invasion was postponed. Finally at the Cairo-Teheran Conference of November 1943 a target date and timetable for the long awaited invasion were established. General Eisenhower was designated as the Supreme Commander of Combined Allied Operations and in February 1944 the Invasion Planning Group was absorbed into Supreme Headquarters Allied Expeditionary Force (SHAEF). The operation finally approved, code named Overlord, was to be the most massive amphibious action of World War II.

Two factors were of crucial concern in the development of Operation Overlord. The first was German troop strength in France, estimated at approximately 59 divisions, including those at garrisons in Belgium and Holland. The second was the ability of the Allies to move the initial invasion force to Europe and maintain it there. This meant that the Allies would have to capture at least one primary port in the initial landings, which the German High Command considered the Achilles' heel of the Allied strategy. It would take time and resources to drive the German armies from occupied areas. The effort would crumble rapidly if denied reinforcements and resupply.

The initial plans for Overlord called for a simultaneous landing of three divisions supported by an airborne landing of divisional strength to cut German lines of communication with the beach areas and to intercept the advance of reinforcements from inland positions during the first few hours of the invasion. Although the basic plan was sound, Eisenhower and

Above: General Eisenhower talks to men of the 101st Airborne Div.

his new assistant in charge of all ground forces for the invasion, General Montgomery, realized that the troop numbers were far too low. They issued a proposal which called for an initial beachhead assault force of five divisions, landed at five separate sites with the support of three airborne divisions which would seize crucial bridges and roads to give flank protection to the landing forces. Eisenhower also believed that the invasion area should be softened by massive, prolonged air bombardment. After the bombers paved the way by creating chaos and destruction of German lines of communication and supply, they could then provide close air support by eliminating coastal defenses and later tactical ground support of the troops. Eisenhower put the command of all Allied strategic and tactical air squadrons into the hands of the invasion force commander, Montgomery, to eliminate the possibility of confusion or error in the coordination of air and ground activities. This caused an angry protest in the Allied air forces, who considered this a blatant attempt to usurp their authority. Eisenhower, who retained the ultimate policy decision, refused to be moved from his position. Allied aircraft had by 1944 won superiority in the skies and he wanted every effort made to ensure that superiority would be used to its fullest potential.

By the time Overlord was nearing execution Germany had approximately 400 aircraft dedicated to the defense of northern France. Eisenhower on the other hand had more than 10,000 aircraft at his disposal. Of this number 3500 were four-engined bombers, 1600 were twin-engined tactical bombers and more than 5000 were fighters. There were also some 2300 transport aircraft, capable of carrying 27,000 paratroopers, and 900 gliders.

reported his belief that von Rundstedt's strategy was wrong. He offered the suggestion that coastal fortifications should be established all along the shoreline to be supported by strong local reserves. Rommel did not feel that von Rundstedt's mobile reserve was strong enough to meet a concerted Allied effort which might occur away from the major ports. Although Rommel agreed with von Rundstedt's belief that the main Allied effort would be made in the area of Dunkirk, he also believed that the Allies would mount secondary, diversionary landings elsewhere which would be large enough to draw valuable German troops and equipment from the main invasion. The Allies had used this diversionary tactic throughout their Mediterranean campaign and Rommel saw no reason for them to change their pattern.

The invasion site became a crucial concern. The beaches had to be adequate to handle the actual landings with port facilities nearby. Other issues such as the proximity of airfields and German troop distribution had also to be considered before a location could be selected. The German command was examining these same issues. Marshal von Rundstedt, commander of German forces in the coastal area, recognized the Allies' need for a viable port to resupply invasion forces. With this in mind he staged his forces in a relatively loose coastal defense supported by a mobile strike force, while concentrating his primary defense forces around such cities as Rotterdam, Le Havre, Cherbourg and the Calais-Dunkirk region, as well as Saint Malo, Brest and Saint Nazaire in Brittany.

In December 1943 as the invasion of Italy was in progress Hitler called for Rommel to inspect the Atlantic defenses and to give his opinion of their condition. After a quick inspection tour Rommel

Allied diversionary tactics followed the pattern expected by the Germans. The Calais-Dunkirk area was so obviously a site that it was immediately discarded for the invasion. However to keep the German command off guard and to foster the belief that the main invasion would be in that area, a ficticious army group was created. Eisenhower placed Patton, whose controversial striking of an enlisted soldier in August 1943 had resulted in his removal from the Mediterranean, in charge of the 'paper army.' The respect the German command felt for Patton's capabilities would be illustrated by the seriousness with which they received information deliberately leaked about Patton's command. Ironically Hitler would hold his Fifteenth Army in reserve waiting for a rash, egotistical general who might never again receive a combat command. The actual site chosen for the landings was the coast of Normandy between the points where the Orne River, which flowed through Caen, met the sea and the beaches just north of

produced the Pluto. This was a novel device capable of pumping essential gasoline supplies through a pipeline laid from England to Normandy on the Channel floor. This invention would prove critical to the success of the Allied operation.

Once the Allies decided on a viable invasion site, the naval aspects of the invasion had to be planned in detail. The invasion fleet would be divided between fighting and transport vessels. More than 1200 ships from seven countries would provide escort and support for the invasion forces. The United States would contribute to this fleet three battleships, three cruisers, thirty-four destroyers and nine minesweepers. Transport vessels would number more than 4000 and would be commanded by the British Admiral Ramsay. In his planning Ramsay decided

Carentan. The location was chosen for many reasons. First because it was considered one of the weakest points of the German defense. The elite German Fifteenth Army had been pulled from the area to Calais and the defending Seventh Army, though possessing many top rank units including SS forces, had been stripped of its armor reserves by the Fifteenth Army. The second surprise for the German command would be provided by Lord Louis Mountbatten of the Royal Navy. Mountbatten was known for his experiments with innovations to aid the fighting soldier. One of his 'minor miracles' was the creation of an artificial harbor to support the invasion. Constructed in England to be towed to France these harbors could handle 6000 tons of supplies daily. Their introduction into the D-Day planning gave credence to the Normandy concept and removed the pressure created by the need for port facilities. In conjunction with his ideas for the artificial harbors, dubbed Mulberry A and B, Mountbatten also

that it made the greatest sense for all American troops to be carried on US vessels commanded by American officers. For this reason Ramsay placed Rear-Admiral Kirk in command of the Western Task Force, whose responsibility it was to deliver the American V and VII Corps to their appointed beaches.

The final invasion plans were approved. Three airborne divisions, two American and one British, would be dropped into the area to hold the flanks and secure crucial areas in preparation for the landings. The invasion fleet would enter the Bay of Seine where the beaches had been divided into an American and a British zone. The American westernmost zone had two designated beaches, Utah and Omaha, which were the responsibility of the US First Army, General Omar Bradley commanding. The eastern British zone had three beach sites, Gold, Juno and Sword. The beaches Gold and Sword would be the responsibility of the British Second Army, while the Canadian 3rd Division would be the first to land at Juno. The Allies had assembled a force for the invasion and liberation of approximately 3,000,000 men. The initial invasion force of 15 divisions would be landed in the first days of the operation. Another 30 divisions would follow from England once the beachheads were secured and the march to recapture France was in progress.

As the scheduled invasion dates approached, bad weather closed in over the Channel. Of the three days chosen, 5, 6 or 7 June, only the nights of 5 and 6 June would provide weather adequate for the crossing. Even then extensive cloud cover and choppy seas were expected. The tides were thought to be normal however and with a degree of luck the operation would proceed as planned. Eisenhower seriously considered postponing the landings, which would have meant a delay of three full weeks. However it was pointed out to him that the men were beginning to suffer from the strain of being confined to bases and aboard ship and that further delays might cause a serious breakdown of morale or breaches in security. Finally on Tuesday 6 June 1944 Eisenhower gave the go-ahead. Operation Overlord was at last underway.

Between 0100 and 0200 hours the lead regiments of the US 82nd and 101st Airborne Divisions were on their way. The 82nd was given the mission of dropping in to take the town and crossroad at Ste Mère Eglise and to secure all bridges in the area to aid troops advancing from Utah. The 101st was assigned to capture the town of Carentan which lay directly inland from Utah and to hold a line along the Douve River. The 101st would keep the area between Utah and Omaha open for the intended link-up and ensure that Utah was not isolated from the other four beachheads. At the same time the British 6th Airborne Division was being dropped on the easternmost flank of the landing zones. American airdrops resulted in chaos and near disaster. Cloud cover made navigation and target location difficult and many of the pilots' instructions had been simply, 'follow the plane ahead of you and drop on signal.' In spite of the fact that the paratroopers were scattered over the surrounding countryside and unnecessary accidental casualties were taken, they succeeded in achieving almost all of their initial objectives. Although the 101st could assemble only 33 percent of its total force into fighting formation it secured the crossroads and bridgeheads assigned to it. Carentan itself was found to be heavily occupied. By morning most of the units were composed of troops from both divisions combined and led by ranking officers and NCOs. As the landings began the 101st defended the beaches from approaching German units, taking more than 1200 casualties by the end of the first day. The 82nd Division, though less scattered, was dropped into a more heavily defended area. Sixty percent of their equipment was lost or destroyed in the initial drop but the division still managed to secure their positions. Later they would be engaged by the German 91st Division and by the

Above: landing craft cluster on Omaha Beach after the initial landings on D-day.

end of the first day they too would lose more than 1200 men. The 82nd would have to fight on alone for two days before making contact with either the 101st or the 4th Infantry Division, which led the assault on Utah.

At 0630 hours on 6 June the first assault waves made their way to the beaches of Normandy. Bradley's Army, composed of the V and VII Corps, approached Utah and Omaha. The 4th Infantry Division of General Collins' VII Corps would be the first to land on Utah. Naval and aerial bombardment of the German defenses preceded the assaults. The 4th Division, whose landing craft were to be launched eight miles off-shore, was forced by the relentless range of the German shore batteries to set out while their parent ships were still 12 miles out to sea. The rough waters made most of the men seasick before they were half way to the shore. As the coast drew near

inland along the Pouppeville Causeway where it would link with elements of the 101st to liberate Ste Mère Eglise. By evening the VII Corps had some 23,000 men and 3500 vehicles on shore. Surprisingly enough the 4th Division had lost only 200 men, thanks to Roosevelt's quick, clear thinking on the beach.

At the other American beachhead the situation would not be as favorable. Off Omaha, as was the case at Utah, the landing craft were put to sea 12 miles out, but the water was rougher in this area and many of the craft were swamped almost immediately. Of a 30 tank battalion of Duplex Drive tanks only two ever reached the shore. The tides played havoc with the assault craft, pushing the eight leading battalions eastward and scattering them along the coast. The 40 minute pre-assault naval bombardment was mismanaged and failed to destroy the German beach defenses. Although it was of little comfort during the initial landings, it would later be discovered that the over-ranged naval gunfire did cause a great deal of damage to the German inland defenses and minefields.

As the first wave of troops landed they were immediately pinned down by murderous machine gun fire. Twenty-five minutes later the second wave landed, only to find the advance troops huddled at the very edge of the shore. Within ten minutes casualties had reduced most units by 25 to 50 percent. Special Army-Navy Engineers sent in to destroy the beach defenseworks could not perform their missions as the German defenses were the only place for the American troops to shelter. Successive waves continued to land with nowhere to go once they reached the shore. Finally General Huebner, the local assault commander, succeeded in halting further landing parties. Navy destroyers maneuvered to within 1000 yards of the shore and began to bombard the German positions. As the 1st Infantry Division began to advance across the 600 yards of open beach, the 29th Infantry Division began making its way to the shore. The situation was so desperate that at one point Bradley considered aborting the Omaha operation and the German defensive units had reported to their headquarters that the invasion in their sector had been repulsed.

By the evening of 6 June despite the loss of 3000 men, 50 tanks, 20 artillery pieces, 50 infantry landing craft and ten larger naval vessels, lead elements of the V Corps had moved two miles inland from Omaha along a front four miles wide. The 2nd Ranger Battalion had also managed to climb the cliffs between Utah and Omaha and silenced the German guns that were creating chaos on the beaches. The 101st Airborne and elements of the VII Corps continued to move inland and secured the surrounding area. The British, though faced with difficult odds, had secured their beaches. D-Day, the Invasion of Normandy, was a success and the liberation of France had begun.

several of the larger landing craft, one of which carried the vital tanks, struck mines and sank. Other tanks, known as Duplex Drive or DD Tanks, which were equipped with flotation devices to let them 'swim' ashore, were having difficulty gaining headway. Several were swamped and the others did not arrive on the beaches until long after the ground troops had begun to move inland.

The landing had become so confused that the 8th Infantry Regiment found itself on the wrong section of the beachhead. Fortunately Brigadier General Theodore Roosevelt Jr had chosen to accompany the men ashore. Rather than attempt to shift the regiment Roosevelt first offered his men encouragement then ordered the following waves to keep coming ashore and began to move directly inland. The error would prove to be a blessing. If the 8th Regiment had landed at its proper position it would have walked directly into machine gun fire from the fortified bunkers which were concentrated on that section of the shore. By the end of that day the 4th Division would be pushing

7 NORMANDY TO VE-DAY

With the Normandy beachheads secured the Allies began to gather their strength for the breakout and advance across Western Europe. The German command nevertheless refused to believe that Normandy was the true invasion site. Hitler, in anticipation of an attack by Patton at Calais, withheld the large armored reserve in the north.

Although the Allied Command had chosen an excellent point for the invasion, the countryside inland would provide the Germans with many defensive positions. This region of Normandy was known as the Bocage and was an area of scenic beauty where small farming plots were separated by thick, high hedgerows. Visibility in most areas was limited to the area between one hedgerow and the next or along the narrow country roads. Rommel recognized that this terrain would present a serious problem to the Allied armor so there was a good chance that a staunch German effort could contain the invasion force. Thus if the Allies actually intended to advance from their position the only route of easy access would be toward Caen. A move on this eastern edge of the Allied front would circumvent the Bocage and give them a clear path to Paris.

Montgomery was equally aware of these conditions and prepared to react by advancing from the center, through the Bocage, between St Lô and Caen. He was preparing to link the five beachheads into one continuous line when the 101st Airborne took Carentan. In doing so they helped to close the gap between Utah and Omaha. The Allied front now stretched along a line 42 miles wide. The strategy as the German command would soon discover was not to advance toward Paris but to capture the Contentin Penninsula on the Allied right flank and thereby capture the port of Cherbourg. The Americans would accomplish this by 27 June, which was advantageous as stormy seas had demolished the artificial harbor off Ste Laurent. During the assault on Cherbourg General Collins introduced an apparatus he called 'the hedge-cutter.' The device was merely a large metal triangle which when attached to the front of tanks allowed them to rip through the hedgerows with relative ease. Collins had seen similar devices during his service in the Pacific at Guadalcanal. Their introduction removed the obstacle that had been

presented by the Bocage.

Although the Allied positions grew stronger each day they were still encircled by the German defenses. It had finally been acknowledged that the Normandy invasion was the main Allied effort and Hitler ordered the reserve armored units to be brought to this front. There was a brief period in which the balance of forces was extremely critical. The German command realized that if the Allies succeeded in breaking through the coastal defenses there might be no way of stopping their advance until the Belgium-Dutch or French-German borders were reached. The relocation of German forces to the Normandy beachhead was causing deep concern in the American command, which wanted to begin the second phase of the invasion immediately. Montgomery believed differently. He wanted to wait until the weakest point in the German line could be found. This was the tactic he had successfully applied at El Alamein, but his critics questioned the validity of his theory in the current situation. Finally Montgomery chose his

Above left: US forces come under fire in the Seine valley near Paris on 23 August 1944. Above and left: house-to-house fighting in St Malo as German troops are cleared from Brittany. Far left: GIs fight their way through the Normandy *bocage* during the break-out from the Cotentin peninsula.

strategy, a combined American and British effort. The British would keep the Germans occupied in the east while the Americans swung from the west in an encircling maneuver against the weaker resistance in that area. German Panzer units broke through to attack the British position. It appeared that the German army was concentrating its primary effort in the British sector, which fitted well into Montgomery's scheme.

As the American units neared St Lô their advance began to stall by 18 July. One week later American bomber strikes against the German positions broke the resistance and Collins was able to begin his offensive on the following day. By 1 August the American units had captured the entire Contentin Penninsula and had swung as far south as Avranches. The American VIII Corps, created from the divisions which had joined the invasion after D-Day, had advanced to a position from which they were ordered to capture Brittany. They accomplished that goal in less than one week, but the main offensive drive was yet to come. This assault was to push south to Le Mans then

swing east. It was given the codename Cobra, as the maneuver resembled a snake drawing back its head to strike. By this time American reinforcements had reached such proportions that two complete armies could be created. General Bradley, commander of the American First Army was promoted to the command of the Twelfth Army Group, supreme field commander for both the armies in Western Europe. Lieutenant General Courtney Hodges took command of the First Army and the newly formed American Third Army was given to Lieutenant General George Patton. Although Patton's return to combat was criticized by many of his peers, both Eisenhower and Bradley realized that if anyone could make Cobra work it was he.

The Cobra strategy was simple. While Montgomery's British forces and Hodges' First Army kept the German troops engaged, Patton's forces were to swing out to encircle and entrap German troops at Falaise. Later a second maneuver was to be executed to trap other German units on the Seine. Again the

German command played into Allied hands by attacking at precisely the point where the Cobra strategy wanted them to be. By 16 August American units in the south and Canadian units from the north had begun to close the noose around Falaise. On 20 August the encirclement was complete and 50,000 German troops were trapped. Remnants of the Fifth and Seventh Panzer Armies made their way rapidly northeast toward the Seine, but Patton reached the river first and the German troops who managed to escape did so only by leaving their equipment behind. Montgomery's original strategy to break the German siege around the Normandy beachheads had been converted into the complete destruction of two full Panzer Armies. The sweep had extended as far south as the Loire River and there was nothing to hamper an American drive to Paris. The rout of Germany's armies had begun.

While the encirclement at Falaise was being made Allied forces struck in southern France. Three divisions of the American Seventh Army, the 3rd, 45th and 36th, commanded by General Patch, combined with one Free French division, landed with minimal resistance between Toulon and Cannes on the French Riviera. The activity of Allied forces in the north and south of France became too great a burden and two days after the invasion of southern France German forces began to withdraw. Allied forces in the north and south of France, particularly Patton's army, were short of supplies. The enemy was in retreat and, although German units occasionally turned to fight, the most deadly enemy in August 1944 was logistics.

The Allies were now in a position to liberate Paris. In fact Patton had swung past the capital in pursuit of German forces. However Eisenhower did not consider Paris to be a primary objective. Although the liberation of the French capital would make great headlines and would be politically advantageous to both Roosevelt and Churchill, Eisenhower knew that once the Allied armies had swept past the Paris garrison it would crumble of its own accord. He saw no reason to waste troops in what could become a monumental battle for that city. Eisenhower would soon discover that his attitude suited the citizens of Paris perfectly. The Paris Liberation Committee wanted desperately to liberate the city themselves and have their revenge on the German occupation forces. On 17 August General De Gaulle asked that the French 2nd Armored Division of Patton's Third Army be given a position on the front opposite Paris. In this way they might serve two important purposes. The French units would have the satisfaction of being the first to enter their capital and the French regulars would be on hand to take German soldiers and collaborators into protective custody. No one wanted the pent-up emotions of the French people to explode into atrocities. By 25 August 1944 Paris was completely in Allied hands.

Right: General George Patton commanded the US Third Army which spearheaded the Normandy breakout.
Far right: troops of the US 28th Infantry Division march down the Champs Elysées after the liberation of Paris.
Below: Parisians scatter as German snipers open fire during the liberation.
Bottom: US troops enter Paris amid scenes of rejoicing.

By September the British had advanced toward Antwerp and the port was considered captured on 4 September, though German troops held positions that made the port inaccessible to Allied shipping. On 7 September the American First Army captured Liège and the V Corps moved into Luxembourg. Further south the French cities of Metz and Nancy were being approached by Patton's army and also by Patch's army as it moved to link with Patton's southern flank. At this point the Allies were several months ahead of their projected timetable. The next major German defensive position was the Siegfried Line, but the Allies were much stronger than they had been the previous month. Although Antwerp was still not open the logistics problems had been solved. Supplies were flowing to the front and Hodges' First Army received so much that he petitioned Eisenhower for permission to open his food stores to the French people.

It was in this atmosphere of Allied superiority and impending German defeat that plans for the most expedient method of conquering Germany were proposed. Eisenhower favored the broad front as a means to keep German forces spread thinly. By maintaining steady pressure along that wide front sooner or later it would collapse. The British command, particularly Montgomery, thought that a concerted effort on the left flank, which was the responsibility of the British, would crack the German line. Once that was done Allied forces could flow through the breach, isolating the German Fifteenth Army and opening the way to the Rhine Valley. Montgomery's contention was that the Reich was near to collapse and his offensive would certainly prove to be the death blow. However Patton, in his desire to continue the advance of his army, argued that Montgomery's strategy would take vital supplies, particularly gasoline, from the Third Army, reducing its role to a mere holding action while Montgomery and the British Army took all the glory.

Fortunately Eisenhower had plans to employ all the armies and a compromise was reached. Although the war effort was a cooperative venture the American generals expected a certain degree of loyalty from Eisenhower. He could not rob them of supplies to satisfy Montgomery's single-handed effort to win the war. And, as one of his aides pointed out to Eisenhower, it would be impossible to deny Patton gasoline. If it was not given to him he would take it. The compromise allowed Montgomery to make his drive in the north with Hodges' First Army moving toward the Ardennes as support, while to the south Patton's army could continue its broad advance. Supplies, especially gasoline, would be evenly distributed according to the need.

With approval received Montgomery laid formal plans for his offensive which would include one of the largest airborne operations of the war. His strategy was based on the fact that the Siegfried Line did not extend into Holland. He proposed to outflank the enemy line by crossing the Rhine at Arnhem. He would have to capture bridges located at two other points along the line of advance. One was at Grave which crossed the Maas River and the other at Nijmegen across the Waal River. An airborne division would be assigned to capture each of the bridges. The XXX Corps would then advance overland to connect the bridgeheads. With these objectives secured, the German Fifteenth Army would be trapped, the German line outflanked and the Ruhr Valley at the mercy of the Allies. Although the final drive would be spread over an area of 60 miles, crossing at least six major canals and waterways, Eisenhower gave Montgomery's plan his final approval. He also put the Allied First Airborne Army at Montgomery's disposal. As part of that army the American 101st Airborne Division was ordered to take Eindhoven and seize the bridges over the Wilhelmina and Willems Canals which would be the first water obstacles in the drive. The American 82nd Airborne Division would be dropped further north to capture the bridges at Grave and Nijmegen. The British 1st Airborne Division would be given the most

Right: US airborne troops examine the wreckage of one of the gliders used in the Nijmegen operation.
Below: a US tank destroyer takes cover behind a knocked-out pillbox.

difficult task, securing the bridges over the Rhine at Arnhem. The XXX British Corps consisted of the Guards Armoured and the 43rd and 50th Divisions. The primary difficulty of the ground operation lay in the fact that the land over which the Corps had to travel was marshy, intersected by canals with only one road over which to advance.

Operation Market Garden, Market for the airborne phase and Garden for the ground phase, began on 17 September 1944 as the three airborne divisions were dropped into their landing zones. The 101st succeeded in taking all but one of its bridges intact and the 82nd also took its objectives except for Nijmegen which was heavily fortified. The British paratroopers dropped at Arnhem soon discovered that Allied Intelligence had been grossly mistaken in its assessment of German troop strength when they were greeted by two SS Panzer Divisions. By 20 September the XXX Corps had successfully linked with the 101st then the 82nd, but lost its momentum several days later. Neither the advancing column nor the Polish Parachute Brigade, which was delayed by bad weather, would arrive in time to save the situation at Arnhem. Of the 9000 men dropped into that sector only 2400 would return. The operation was declared ended on 26 September after heavy losses to all divisions and the surrender of the 1st Airborne Division. Montgomery is quoted as having said that the operation was indeed a success, but it had been flawed by attempting to gain 'one bridge too far.'

October and November brought continued pressure to force the German withdrawal though the pace had slowed considerably. The American Ninth Army arrived in October through the captured port at Brest and took up a position on the front between Hodge's First and Patton's Third Armies. General Patch had taken a position on Patton's right flank leading the 6th Army Group, which consisted of the American

Seventh Army and the French First Army. Although Patton had advanced to Lorraine, near the German border, his progress was severely hampered by intolerable weather. The hope that the war would be over by Christmas had vanished in the face of Montgomery's fiasco on the northern front and the stiffening German resistance in defense of their homeland. December was also a time when many American units were being rotated to and from the front to give the soldiers a well deserved rest in the rear areas.

Although the fronts had become static, plans were being made for what many believed would be the last offensive against Germany. Eisenhower was optimistic. The logistic situation had been solved as ports fell to the Allies. Nothing was considered critically short and stockpiles were appearing along the front as more than one million tons of supplies had been moved to forward areas. Eisenhower modified his broad front policy, making plans for an Allied offensive early in 1945. It was then that Hitler ordered what no one had considered possible; a major counteroffensive in the Ardennes. It had been there that the German armies had initiated their advance against the Channel ports five years earlier. Apparently the German command believed that a repetition of that former offensive would put the Allied position in serious jeopardy. The attack began on 16 December 1944. The sky was overcast and fog was prevalent, a condition which weather reports indicated would last for several more days. Thus not only did the German assault have the element of surprise but the inclement weather would keep Allied aircraft from lending its support. The German command had chosen its point of attack well, striking at the critical point where Bradley's and Montgomery's forces joined.

The weight of the attack was awesome. The Allied line included the 99th Infantry Division on the

northernmost flank. Next on the line was the 14th Armored Cavalry Regiment, then the 106th Infantry Division, a completely inexperienced unit. At the time of the attack the 106th did not even have its armored battalion attached to lend support. A large portion of this division was captured three days later and many men were shot by their captors. On the 106th's southern flank was the 28th Infantry Division which had been sent to the Ardennes to rest and recuperate fighting it had seen in November. Further south was the 9th Armored Division, which though inexperienced was well equipped. Each of these units had been sent to the Ardennes to rest and recouperate or to gain limited combat experience. Worse yet the Allied command had been in the process of rotating troops when the German attack came.

The situation rapidly degenerated into confusion. The chaos of troop movements was further compounded when English speaking German infiltrators

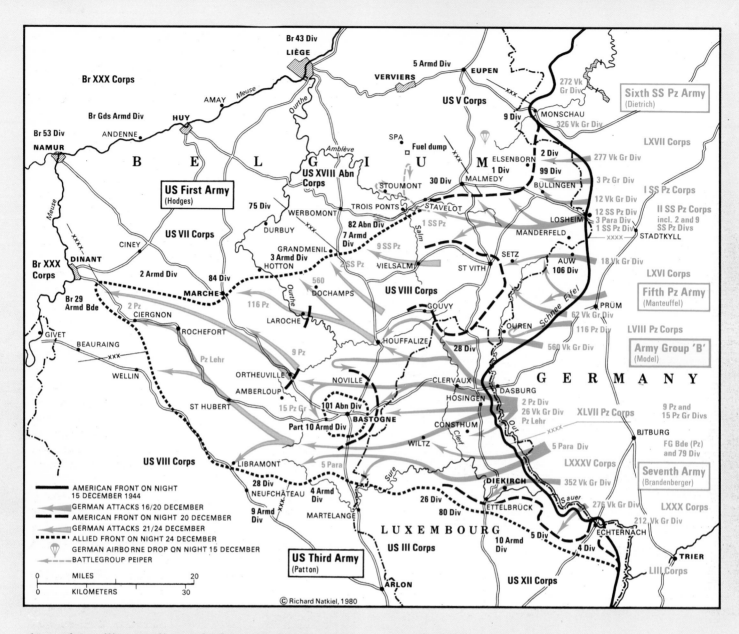

dressed as military police and other military personnel driving American vehicles cut telephone lines, changed roadsigns and generally undermined American efforts to stabilize the situation. For the Americans what would become known as the Battle of the Bulge would have two important aspects: the defense of Bastogne and the Patton offensive. On 19 December the 101st Division took up a position at the strategic crossroad at Bastogne. There they fought the German forces to a stalemate despite overwhelming odds. In fact the surrounded 101st was given up for lost by the Allied Command. On 22 December the German commander offered the 101st surrender terms to which the American commander General McAuliffe is said to have responded, 'Nuts!' That reply, whether mis-quoted or not, became a symbol of the American fighting spirit in World War II. The following day the weather broke and air support to Bastogne was given priority. The 101st held on until 26 December when Patton's 4th Armored Division moved in to relieve

the defenders.

Although American and British forces brought pressure to bear on the northern flank of the bulge it was Patton who broke the German attack. Patton accomplished the seemingly impossible when he pulled his entire Third Army out of the line and in less than 48 hours altered course by 90 degrees and moved 15,000 vehicles 75 miles in some of the worst conditions seen in the war. It was one of the most magnificent maneuvers recorded in warfare and it clearly illustrated that the American citizen-soldier could perform as well if not better than their professional army counterparts.

When the Battle of the Bulge ended a great Allied victory had been achieved but once again a rift developed between American and British generals. Patton wanted to counterattack immediately, which he would, but Montgomery wanted to take things more slowly letting the German army wear itself out before moving in for the kill. In February the

Above left: a map of the German Ardennes offensive, December 1944.
Above: Czech citizens welcome advanced units of Patton's Third Army as they advance towards Prague in May 1945.

explosive fuses. The bridge allowed American troops to cross the Rhine only 12 miles from Bonn. When Hitler discovered that the Ludendorff Bridge had been permitted to fall into American hands he removed von Rundstedt and brought Kesselring from Italy to take command of the defense of Germany. The major who had been sent to destroy the bridge was arrested and shot for treason. The bridge would collapse of its own accord several days later, but it had already served its purpose for the Allied advance.

Further south Patton crossed the Rhine at Oppenheim. Germany lay wide open before him. In the last weeks of March Allied forces surrounded the Ruhr Valley with the British approaching from the north as the Americans swung up from the south. Germany had lost nearly 250,000 men attempting to keep the Allies from crossing the Rhine. This had now been accomplished and Eisenhower shifted the focus of Allied advance to central Germany. This was done to abide by the agreement made between Roosevelt and Stalin which gave Soviet troops the right of capturing Berlin.

On 12 April 1945 with victory so close the United States reeled momentarily with the unbelieveable news that President Franklin Delano Roosevelt was dead. The nation went into mourning and those who respected the great statesman would deeply regret that he did not live to see America's fighting men come home in triumph.

By 18 April 300,000 German troops from Army Group B had surrendered to the Allies. In fact groups of German soldiers flocked to the Western Front so that they would not have to surrender to the Russians and their commander General Model committed suicide. The Allies were now moving approximately 40 miles per day. On 25 April American and Russian troops met for the first time near Leipzig and Patton was in Czechoslovakia. The remainder of April was spent clearing German forces from Holland, which they still occupied. Hamburg and Lubeck were finally taken by 3 May.

The first week of May brought a rapid succession of events. On 1 May Adolf Hitler committed suicide when he finally admitted that the Third Reich was no more. On 2 May Berlin and one million German troops surrendered. By 4 May the Seventh Army was at the Brenner Pass preparing to meet lead elements of the American Fifth Army moving north from Italy. Finally on 7 May Admiral Doenitz, who had taken command after Hitler's death, entered into peace negotiations. On 8 May 1945 an official cessation of all hostilities in Europe was ordered. The United States had seen the war in Europe to an end and could now take its role in establishing the peace in accordance with the aggrements of the Yalta Conference. The nation would then have to turn its full attention to the Pacific. Only then could the United States be at peace.

American First Army, which had been attached to Montgomery's command, was released and given the task of seizing the dam on the River Aachen. It was to be a joint American-Canadian operation. Although the German area forces stopped the American advance by sabotaging the bridge the Canadians were eventually to rendezvous in March. By that time all German resistance west of the Rhine had collapsed. The First Army moved into Cologne as Patton and Patch swept through the Palatinate region of Germany, encircling the remnants of the German Seventh Army.

On 7 March the 9th Armored Division of the First Army discovered that the Ludendorff Bridge at Remagen was intact though damaged. American engineers managed to foil German efforts to demolish the bridge by crawling underneath the structure to cut

INDEX

Acknowledgments

The author would like to thank Adrian Hodgkins, the designer, Penny Murphy who compiled the index and Richard Natkiel who prepared the maps. The following agencies supplied the illustrations.

Bison Picture Library: pp 7, 24–25
Bundesarchiv: p 12
Ian Hogg: pp 19, 20 (bottom)
Imperial War Museum: pp 36, 37, 45, 46, 48
Library of Congress: p 9
National Archives: pp 14, 31 (top), 43, 44, 50, 50–51 (lower), 52–53, 54
Map © Richard Natkiel: pp 31, 42, 62
Robert Hunt Library: p 31 (bottom)
USAF: pp 9 (inset), 27–29
US Army: pp 10, 11, 15, 17, 20 (upper two), 21, 30, 32 (center), 35, 41 (lower), 42–43, 46–47, 49, 50–51 (upper), 51, 55–57, 59–61, 63
US Navy: pp 6, 22, 23, 32 (bottom), 38–39, 40, 41 (upper)